from habitual sexual sin and shame and live in life-giving, soul-satisfying sexual purity."

Candice Watters, wife; mom; and author

"Transforming. Hopeful. Timely. Freeing. After reading this book, I personally found sexual freedom in areas I didn't even know I struggled with. I recommend this book for any daughter, wife, sister, mom, or friend—no matter her age!"

Alyssa Stephens, daughter; big sister; and longtime GirlDefined fan

"Finally, a book that deals with sexuality in a gracious, tactful, and biblical way. Kristen and Bethany are refreshingly candid and unashamedly scriptural as they teach why God created us with sexual desires and what to do about it. This book offers hope for every girl who has ever wondered if she is the only one who struggles with lust, freedom from slavery to her desires, and the truth about God's wonderful design for sexuality. Best of all, in these pages are dozens of Scriptures and practical truths to guide young women into a life of true sexual freedom—freedom to live according to God's design."

Allison Bontrager, blogger at *From Allison*

"One question: Where was this book all my life? Kristen and Bethany have done it again. With tender love yet firm conviction, they give us another installment of truth. Do yourself a favor and savor this book. Let it sink in deeply and then pass it along. You're never too far gone that God can't redeem any and every area of your life. This book (along with God's Word) is a great starting point toward healing and redemption."

Crystal Navarro, simply a flawed reflection of a perfect Jesus and a GirlDefined supporter

D0006597

"I adore these authors! Kristen and Bethany dive headfirst into some of the most pressing topics of our day: sex, purity, identity, marriage, and more. The message of God-defined sexuality is one every woman needs."

Dannah Gresh, author of *And the Bride Wore White*

"Making sense of your sexuality may be a huge roadblock for you as a young Christian woman. Kristen and Bethany are compassionate friends who will encourage you in this journey! In *Sex, Purity, and the Longings of a Girl's Heart*, they offer hope, practical advice, and godly wisdom."

Dr. Juli Slattery, cofounder of Authentic Intimacy; author of *Rethinking Sexuality*

"In a world riddled with sexual confusion, brokenness, and pain, I rejoice that voices like Kristen's and Bethany's are helping young women find their way—His way—and pointing them to the redeeming love and grace of Christ."

Nancy DeMoss Wolgemuth, author; teacher/host of *Revive Our Hearts*

"The sexual struggles and temptations of 'good' Christian girls are often kept in the dark. Kristen and Bethany openly share their personal journeys in an honest and refreshing way. This book is chock-full of solid, practical advice and is a great resource for every woman who longs to embrace a higher and more beautiful godly vision for sexuality."

Mary A. Kassian, author of *Girls Gone Wise*

"Our culture has hopelessly distorted sexuality, but this book shines a spotlight on God's original design for it. With transparency and grace, Kristen and Bethany share their own journeys to sexual purity, boldly expose lies, and encourage young women that there *is* a better way. Not ones to shy away from gritty topics, they tackle tough questions with biblical truth as they paint a beautiful picture of God's good design for sex and challenge us to seek the One Who can ultimately satisfy the longings of our hearts. You'll close the cover of this book challenged, inspired, and equipped to walk in purity—even in a culture that's anything but pure."

Sara Barratt, author; speaker; and lead editor for TheRebelution.com

"This is the book my generation needs. In a culture constantly broadcasting distorted and conflicting messages about sex, we need biblical truth to counteract the lies we hear. Bethany and Kristen graciously, humbly, and wisely help us navigate these complex issues as they point us to God's Word. Every twenty first–century girl needs to read this!"

Jaquelle Crowe, author of *This Changes Everything*

"Outstanding! Kristen and Bethany take on a difficult topic with robust grace, authentic transparency, and biblical clarity. Every girl needs to read this book."

Sean and Jenny Perron, counselors; authors; and director of operations at the Association of Certified Biblical Counselors (Sean)

"Somewhere between our culture's in-your-face messages about sex and the church's awkward silence, there's *Sex, Purity, and the Longings of a Girl's Heart*. As someone who longs to see this generation of young women walking in freedom, I can't champion this book loud enough. Bethany and Kristen remind us that sexuality is broken, but wholeness is possible when we choose to look for answers in the ultimate relationship manual—the Word of God."

Erin Davis, author; blogger; Bible teacher; and member of the GirlDefined Fan Club

"Kristen and Bethany use their own experiences to show that sexuality done the world's way isn't freedom; it's slavery. They challenge readers to the risky work of getting down into our brokenness, but Kristen and Bethany write with grace and truth, keeping the focus on the One who sets us free. They offer powerful help from the Word of God, the Spirit of Christ, and the saving power of the cross to break free

Sex, Purity, and the longings of a Girl's Heart.

DISCOVERING THE BEAUTY AND FREEDOM OF GOD-DEFINED SEXUALITY

KRISTEN CLARK AND BETHANY BEAL

BakerBooks

a division of Baker Publishing Group
Grand Rapids, Michigan

© 2019 by Kristen Clark and Bethany Beal

Published by Baker Books
a division of Baker Publishing Group
PO Box 6287, Grand Rapids, MI 49516-6287
www.bakerbooks.com

Printed in the United States of America

ISBN 978-0-8010-7557-5

Library of Congress Cataloging-in-Publication Control Number: 2018048916

In keeping with biblical principles of creation stewardship, Baker Publishing Group advocates the responsible use of our natural resources. As a member of the Green Press Initiative, our company uses recycled paper when possible. The text paper of this book is composed in part of post-consumer waste.

19 20 21 22 23 24 25   7 6 5 4 3 2 1

To the GirlDefined Sisterhood around the world—
thank you for encouraging us to write *this* book.
We pray it transforms your life for God's glory.

CONTENTS

Contents

Part one

Broken Sexuality

1. WE'RE ALL SEXUALLY BROKEN

This magazine was unlike anything I (Bethany) had ever seen before in my short eight years of life. I stared down at its pages flopping in the wind. The once-glossy cover was dirty and worn, as though one too many cars had run over it. But the images. *What was this?* Looking up, I saw ten-year-old Kristen walking toward me on the sidewalk. "Hey, come here," I said to her in a half whisper. "I found something really interesting."

Kristen hurried toward me. "What is it?" she asked.

"I don't know," I responded.

Once Kristen reached me, she looked down at the magazine lying at my feet. Like a natural big sister, she picked it up without hesitation. After staring at the cover for several seconds, she flipped through the crumpled pages. Looking at me with a nervous face, she quietly said, "C'mon, let's go inside." She rolled the magazine up in her hands and we quietly went inside the house. Once we were in one of the bedrooms with the door shut, Kristen dropped the magazine on the floor. We both stood there silently for several minutes. We weren't sure what to do. After gaining some courage, we began to flip through the pages.

"I don't understand what's happening here," I said to Kristen while pausing on one of the full-page images.

"I'm not sure either," she said.

Kristen and I—innocent girls—were being exposed to pornographic images for the first time in our lives. Our little hearts beat faster. Although we didn't understand the images we were seeing, we knew something wasn't right.

After several more minutes passed, Kristen suddenly shut the magazine and said, "We need to get rid of this."

"Yeah, I think so too," I said as I stood up. With sweaty palms, we checked the hallway, quickly dashed outside, and ran down the sidewalk. The fresh air and bright sunshine felt good.

"Here!" Kristen said, suddenly stopping. We were four houses down from our home. Standing near our neighbor's large brick mailbox, she started digging in the ground with her hands.

"Help me!" she said in a whispered panic.

"What are we doing? Why are you dig—oh! You're going to bury it!"

Jumping on the ground to help her, I ripped up that rock-infested dirt as fast as I could. I never wanted to see those strange images again. Once the hole was big enough, we folded the magazine into fourths and laid it inside. Working as a team, we piled the dirt back into the hole. With our hands slightly bleeding and our nails jammed with dirt, we stood back.

We looked at our little pile. The tiny dirt mound resembled a miniature gravesite.

We felt free. That strange magazine had made us feel weird. Wiping our dirty hands on our floral T-shirts, we headed back to the house. Our secret would remain as buried as that magazine for the next decade.

Romance Novels and Sexual Desires

My (Bethany's) unsolicited exposure to pornographic content that day didn't launch me into a sudden life-altering addiction, but it did launch me into something else. Questions. Confusion. Curiosities. Without my even realizing what was happening, my perspective on sexuality was being subtly influenced in ways it never had been before.

As I grew a little older, I became acutely aware of the images and messages I saw around me. I saw the words *Your Best Sex Now* displayed in bold letters across the top of a magazine at the grocery store. *Sexy Dancers Every Night!* caught my eye on a nightclub sign. *Passion and Love* were displayed in red font across the top of an erotic romance novel.

I saw. I observed. My little mind was curious.

As I grew into a teenager, I noticed something else changing. My *desires*. Without warning, I began experiencing sexual desires and longings. My imagination wandered into fantasies that had been foreign to me previously. I was attracted to boys in new and exhilarating ways.

One summer during my mid-teen years, I started working at a Christian bookstore. It wasn't long before I discovered the romance novel section. Yep, I was immediately hooked. Despite the fact that these books were only mild "Christian" romance novels, they had me fantasizing about romance and sexual experiences just the same. These novels appealed to something deep within me. Longings. Curiosities.

I often wondered, *Are these good feelings or bad feelings? Am I normal or weird?* I wasn't sure what to do with my newly awakened desires, so I just kept them to myself.

15

Near the end of the summer, another book at the bookstore caught my eye—a Christian book on the topic of purity. For the first time, I caught a glimpse of God's bigger picture for my heart and my inner sexual desires. Although the book helped me understand a little bit more about God's design for my sexuality, it didn't make my longings go away. I still wrestled with lustful thoughts. Toggling somewhere between lust and purity, I wanted to do the right thing. I wanted to honor God but wasn't sure just how to do that yet.

Drooling over a Hot Tamale

My (Kristen's) experiences growing up were similar to Bethany's, but I had some unique twists and turns. My exposure to that magazine left images stamped on my mind. I couldn't get them out. They flashed before my eyes at the most unsuspecting moments. I felt too embarrassed to ask my parents about what I had seen, but I desperately wanted to know more. I had questions. A lot of them. I was the kid who always asked *why* about everything. Well, everything except sex. That topic seemed scary for some reason, but I still wanted answers. My little mind was pondering big things—things I never told anyone about.

I soon discovered my own palette of sexual desires and longings. Even before I hit puberty, I discovered masturbation. As an eleven-year-old girl, I had no idea what I was doing. But it seemed good. It felt natural (more on that in the chapters to come).

My little imagination was bombarded with sexualized thoughts too.

During my teen years, my thoughts turned from imaginary situations to scenarios with real guys. I remember meeting this one guy and thinking he was the hottest tamale on the planet. His glances in my direction communicated that he felt the same way about me. We ended up chatting for a few minutes. My inner self was drooling. After parting ways, I did what any good trying-to-play-it-cool girl would do—I stalked him on social media. As I scrolled through his past albums (gotta scout the archives), I discovered this guy was an even hotter tamale online! I wouldn't have called it lust back then, but that's exactly what was happening in my heart. I drooled over his shirtless photos. My eyes lingered on his chiseled muscles. My mind wandered into sexual places. In the privacy of my room and heart, I indulged in my lust. I felt bad but wasn't sure what to do. Deep inside, I knew my thoughts didn't honor God; but since I wasn't physically acting on them, I brushed it off as no big deal.

In the privacy of my room and heart, I indulged in my lust.

I convinced myself that being pure was more about what I looked like on the outside than what I was feeling on the inside.

Gold-Star Christian Girls

Even though the two of us grew up in a great Christian home, we wrestled with sexual sin and temptation just like anybody else. Our secret desires were often warped and self-centered. Our thoughts were sometimes full of lust. As regular church and Sunday school attendees, we heard multiple talks on purity. We read numerous books on God's design for love and purity. We studied our Bibles and saw that God called us to "flee from sexual immorality" (1 Cor. 6:18), but we still struggled. We didn't understand God's bigger purpose for our sexuality.

As we entered our later teen years, we both embraced the idea of saving sex for marriage, but we didn't fully understand *why* doing so was important. We were on board with pursuing purity but thought it was more about avoiding consequences than striving to honor God. We sincerely wanted to be devoted Christians, but our focus was more on good works than humbly relying on God's grace and strength to change us.

Even though we wrestled with temptation and lust, we still saw ourselves as really good Christian girls. Since we had never committed any of the "big bad Church sins," we assumed we were fairly righteous. Without ever saying it out loud, we both viewed ourselves as gold-star Christian girls.

We're All Sexually Broken

As "good" as the two of us thought we were at one point, God didn't leave us in that prideful state. Being the gracious Father that He is, He helped us realize our wrong perspective. That realization wasn't an overnight thing though. It was a process. And it still is. Over the next few years, God graciously helped us see our own tarnishes. We weren't as shiny as we had thought. We weren't as good as we had thought. The sexual sin in our hearts was just as wrong as any outward sexual sin. We began to see that, in God's eyes, even the smallest distortion of righteousness is still a distortion. It misses the mark of true holiness. Our problem wasn't an isolated sin issue that popped up here and there; it was a sinful *condition* that permeated our entire being. We were born with an indwelling sin nature that impacted every area of our lives and ultimately separated us from a holy and righteous God (see Rom. 7:18; John 14:6).

Now, as women in our thirties, we have a completely different perspective. Our eyes have been opened to the reality and depth of our sin and we've discovered something profound. We were never actually *good*. Not even close. Our hearts were never whole—they were broken. Our desires were never perfect because they were always distorted by our sinful condition.

We've now realized, more than ever, that we desperately need Jesus. We need God's forgiveness in our lives just as much as "the world" does. We need His righteousness to cover our sin. Thankfully, Jesus died on the cross and rose again to conquer the power of sin and to provide a way for us to have a relationship with God. He took the punishment that we rightly deserved in order to satisfy the just wrath of God (Rom. 5:9; 1 John 4:12). By accepting Jesus's payment on our behalf, we can stand forgiven before God (more on this in chapter 5). As Jesus changes our hearts from the inside out, He transforms our desires from impure ones to righteous ones. Instead of strutting around in self-righteousness, we are now learning to walk in humble reliance on Him. We need His grace and strength every single day.

Our hearts were never whole—they were broken.

Our friend Dr. Juli Slattery, who is a respected expert on topics regarding biblical sexuality, made the statement that "we are all sexually broken."[1] As we've grown in our understanding of God's design for our sexuality, we've realized she's right. People aren't either sexually "whole" or sexually "broken." The reality is, we're *all* sexually broken. Every one of us. And as we've talked to other Christians (new and seasoned), they've said the same thing about themselves.

We've all experienced some form of sexual struggle or distortion due to sin. None of us are completely whole. None of us are completely pure. None of us experience God's perfect design for our sexuality as He originally intended. Regardless of our background, upbringing, race, or age, sexual brokenness is something we all face. Sure, it will look different for each of us. But it's something we all have to deal with. Whether we struggle with a secret sin, occasional lust, sexual promiscuity, homosexual desires, pornography addiction, masturbation, or something else, one thing is clear: we, as women, are sexually broken.

Over the past few years, we've received thousands of emails from women like you who have shared their stories of sexual brokenness. In preparing to write this book, we did a survey through GirlDefined.com and asked 450 Christian women specific questions regarding their sexual struggles. Here are what a few of them had to say (to protect their privacy, the names have been omitted):

"I have been struggling with porn for a while now, and I don't know what to do. I'm ashamed and scared of letting my secret out. I need help, but I can't get it because I'm too ashamed to tell others."

"I was a victim of several sexually abusive situations as a young girl. I've had a lot of issues as a result and have spent most of my adult life fighting addiction and depression."

"I struggle with same-sex attraction to women. This has been an issue in my life for as long as I can remember. If it's so wrong, why doesn't God take my desires away?!"

"My mind is a war zone. Lust is almost constantly invading my thoughts."

These are real Christian women. Struggling. Hurting. Each one of them is experiencing some form of sexual brokenness.

Whether she is committing a sin or a sin is being committed against her, each woman is suffering.

If you had to add your own struggles to the bottom of that list, what would you say? As you think about your past and present, how has your own sexuality been marred by sin? Sometimes it's easy for us to think we're the only ones struggling, but we're not. Each one of us is carrying our own burdens. Each one of us is wrestling with our own sexual brokenness. Each one of us is in desperate need of sexual *restoration*.

The Journey That Shaped You

From the time you were born until now, you've been on a journey. As you've traveled through the days, weeks, months, and years of your life, you've learned things. You've experienced things. You've been exposed to things. You've chosen things. And whether or not you realize it, you've formed your worldview of sexuality as a result of these things.

In addition to your personal experiences, you've also been shaped by the society around you. And sadly, since the loudest voice that defines sexuality is a society's culture, your perspective about sex has most likely been influenced by it.

In her book *Rethinking Sexuality*, Dr. Slattery writes, "One day it dawned on me. We have been sexually discipled by the world. What I mean is that we have been taught to see sexuality from the world's narrative. I find that most Christians are more familiar with how to view sexuality through a cultural lens than with a biblical perspective."[2]

The world has a lot to say about our sexuality. It has a loud voice too. From popular movies to music to books to

billboards to magazines to the internet—sexual discipleship is happening everywhere. And the messages of pop
culture are bold: Be free. Have sex. Mess
around. Follow your heart. Do what
feels good. Do it now.

The world has a lot to say about our sexuality.

As you think back on your personal journey, what connections can
you make regarding pop culture's
influence on your understanding of
sexuality—whether negative or positive? What has shaped your beliefs about
sex? What has been most influential in your life?

So much of the confusion surrounding our sexuality is
a result of being discipled by the world. The only way to
redeem our sexuality is to turn back to the One who created us. Instead of continuing to listen to the world and
our sinful hearts, we need to be discipled by the One who
designed us. The One who loves us and created us. The
One who understands our sexuality and has a good and
beautiful plan for it.

The two of us don't know your personal journey or struggles. We don't know the confusion and pain in your life. But
God does. He knows and He cares deeply. He sees you and
He loves you. He knows that everything you've experienced,
done, seen, heard, and learned has brought you to this point
today. And you know what? He wants to forgive your past
(see 1 John 1:9). He wants to redeem your future (see Isa.
61:3). He wants to renew your heart and mind (see Rom.
12:2). He wants to free you from habitual sin (see Ps. 51:10).
He wants to reclaim your understanding of sexuality (see
2 Tim. 2:21). He wants to transform your brokenness into
beauty for His glory.

Why We Wrote This Book

God intentionally created each one of us to be sexual beings. From the beginning of time, He made us with sexual desires. He designed us this way on purpose and for a purpose. He's not a killjoy in the sky who wants to squash our sexual feelings. He's a loving Creator who wants to steer our affections in the right direction. Out of love, He's given us beautiful parameters for how to embrace our sexuality in the right ways. He created us as sexual beings to teach us spiritual truths about Himself. He created us with an ache for intimacy to draw us into an authentic relationship with Him. He created us to be relational because He is relational. He created us to be ultimately and completely satisfied in Him.

God intentionally created each one of us to be sexual beings.

The more we chase after God's good design, the more the confusion will clear up. The more we chase after our Savior, the more He will satisfy us in ways nothing on this earth ever could.

As you begin a new phase of your journey through the pages of this book, here's what you'll discover:

- A biblical understanding of your sexuality
- God's good design for love, passion, and sex
- Why your longings for intimacy are actually a good thing
- How to conquer lust in your life
- What God's Word teaches about porn, masturbation, and erotica
- How to deal with secret sexual struggles

- Practical help for embracing a heart of purity
- How to find ultimate satisfaction in Jesus
- Much more

Regardless of where you've been or what you're facing today, the two of us are excited you're reading this book. We pray that the truths of God's Word transform your life the way they have ours.

Instead of settling for a counterfeit version of sexuality, it's time to pursue the truth. Instead of falling prey to cheap thrills and fleeting pleasures, it's time to fight for what lasts. Instead of staying stuck in secret sin and darkness, it's time to be free.

It's time to embrace your sexuality as the Creator intended. With passion, purpose, and purity. *All for His glory.*

2. LUST: A GIRL'S PROBLEM TOO

Katie looked nervous. Almost scared. I (Kristen) wondered what was going through her mind. She walked a little closer and then hesitated. She looked as though she had changed her mind and was going to turn around. Before she had a chance to leave, I made eye contact with her and gave her a warm and reassuring smile. This was all it took to let her know that I cared about her. With her eyes now filled with tears and mascara running down her face, I pulled her into a great big hug. The two of us stood there for several minutes as she sobbed. Whatever was going on inside her mind had obviously been kept under lock and key for quite some time.

The moment of truth had finally come for Katie.

Over the next hour, Katie shared her story of struggle and shame. Years and years of pain were finally coming to the surface. For the first time ever, she confessed her multiyear battle with porn. As soon as Katie brought this secret into the light, she felt as though a huge weight had been lifted from her shoulders. This was no longer her battle to fight alone. She now had reinforcements in the fight.

Katie and I spent some amazing time together that day. We prayed, we cried, and we created a serious battle plan that would help her walk in grace, forgiveness, and victory from that moment forward. After Katie wiped the final tears from her eyes, I looked at her and gently asked why she had waited so many years to share about her battle with porn. Her answer was simple and yet deeply saddening. She said, "I always felt like lust was a guy problem, not a girl problem. I assumed I was the only girl who struggled with porn, so I kept it a deep, dark secret. It wasn't until I heard you share about your secret struggles with masturbation that I finally felt free to share about my sexual struggles. Today was the first time I realized that I wasn't the only girl who struggled with lust."

Katie's story is just one of the many real-life stories women have shared with the two of us. Over the years, we've heard from hundreds of women who've bravely reached out to us for help with their sexual struggles. While talking with these women, we often ask why they waited so long to reach out. Why they kept silent.

Their response is almost always the same: "I felt like I was the only woman who struggled with lust. There was no way I was going to share about my struggles when I felt like nobody else could relate."

That's why they kept silent.

"I felt like I was the only woman who struggled with lust."

Each one of these women concluded that they were the only one—the only female in the world who struggled with lust. Instead of opening up and sharing about their issues, many of them felt they must walk the journey alone. If they were the only woman who struggled with lust, then they must fight the battle on their own. How could they possibly open up and share if nobody else could relate?

Despite the fact that many of us have felt as though we're the only ones who struggle with lust, we're anything but alone. Here's what a few Christian women had to say about lust:

"Lust is something I struggle with on a daily basis."

"Lust has been a struggle in both my singleness and my dating relationships."

"Lust is a problem almost all girls struggle with but is so infrequently talked about in the Church."

"Lust is not spoken about. We girls are confused and frustrated. We need someone to talk frankly with and to help us understand what the Bible says about this issue and how we can live pure lives before the Lord physically as well as mentally and emotionally."

These women were honest and willing to put themselves out there. To them, lust is 100 percent a girl problem too. No doubt about it.

To change the narrative about lust, we need to get honest with ourselves and with others. We need to begin talking about our struggles and share openly with other women. Staying silent on the issue will only compound the problem.

If lust stays under the false banner of being a "guy-only" issue, women will continue to stay silent in their bondage. We, as women, will remain alone and isolated in the battle.

Not a Guy Problem—a Human Problem

Having grown up in the Church and in a Christian family, the two of us agree that lust is most often presented as a guy issue. Guys get the Bible studies on battling lust. Guys get the weekend retreats on purity and guarding their eyes. Guys get the weekly accountability groups regarding their sexual struggles. But women in today's society may find it harder to access these same kinds of resources and opportunities. Thankfully, this is slowly changing.

More and more women are expressing concerns similar to the ones quoted above and opening up and asking for help. Because of that, we're slowly seeing the tides change from lust being portrayed as a guy problem to lust being portrayed as a human problem.

In a sermon titled "Battling the Unbelief of Lust," pastor John Piper describes the issue of lust this way: "Sexual desire in itself is good. God made it in the beginning. It has its proper place. But it was made to be governed or regulated or guided by two concerns: honor toward the other person and holiness toward God. Lust is what that sexual desire becomes when that honor and that holiness are missing from it."[1]

The two words he uses to describe lust are extremely helpful: *honor* and *holiness*. When our sexual desires and longings are void of honor toward the other person and void of holiness toward God, we end up with lust. When we fantasize about a hot guy who is not our husband, we're not honoring him and we're not acting in holiness toward God. We're lusting when we behave that way. Plain and simple. In the same way, when a guy looks at a woman and undresses her in his mind, he is not honoring her and he is not acting in holiness toward God. He is lusting. At the root of both these scenarios is one thing: sexual sin. The way sexual sin manifests itself in men and women may look a little different, but the heart motive is the same. That's because both men and women crave and desire sex. Both genders are created to be sexual by design.

Despite what you may currently think about your own sexuality or the way sexuality is portrayed in culture, men and women are designed to be sexual. Way back in the Garden of Eden, "God created mankind in his own image, in the image of God he created them; male and female he created them" (Gen. 1:27 NIV). Although He made them unique and different as male and female, one thing was the same. They were both very much sexual beings. They both had the ability to enjoy sexual intimacy and to crave and desire sex.

Both genders are created to be sexual by design.

Fast-forward several thousand years, and we now have a world full of Adam and Eve's descendants. Think about it. God created one male and one female. In the perfect Garden, we can assume they had passionate intimacy (designed and given to them by God as an amazing aspect of their humanity), which produced children. We, as twenty-first-century women, are on this earth as a result of that initial sexual relationship. We're the result of two sexual beings coming together and creating new life.

Although we live in an era much different from Adam and Eve's, we're very much like them. We're just as sexual as our greatest grandmother Eve, because God designed us to be that way.

MEN AND WOMEN: WHAT'S THE DIFFERENCE?

Let's unpack a few of the major differences between men and women. These simple explanations will help you better understand the way you tick and the way men tick. They will also help you recognize the root motives of your lust compared to the root motives of a man's lust. (Keep in mind these are stereotypical differences. That means they are not always 100 percent true for every man and every woman.)

Men

- Men are created to pursue and often find the pursuit of a woman stimulating.
- Men are sexually aroused by what they see (which is why women often wear lingerie).
- Men typically find the physical aspect of a relationship more pleasurable than the emotional.
- Men long to be desired sexually by their wives. This affirms their masculinity and lets them know they are valued and respected.
- Men are physically designed to give to the woman in a sexual relationship. A man's physical design is only a mere reflection of his overall distinct role.

Women

- Women are created to respond and often find being pursued by a man very stimulating.
- Women are sexually aroused by touch and want to be desirable and touchable (this is one of the reasons women enjoy wearing lingerie).
- Women typically enjoy physical pleasure most when it's in conjunction with emotional closeness.
- Women long to be desired relationally by their husbands. This affirms their femininity and lets them know they are loved and cherished.
- Women are physically designed to receive from the man in a sexual relationship. A woman's physical design is only a mere reflection of her overall distinct role.

This simple comparison is designed to showcase two specific things about men and women: 1. Men and women typically give love and receive love differently. 2. Men and women are both sexual by design. It's important to note that although men and women operate differently, they are both very much sexual to the core of their beings. We, as women, need to recognize our unique sexual design so we can better face the battle of lust in our everyday lives.

Men and women typically give love and receive love differently.

We're All in This Together

Several years ago, the two of us were discussing the theme for our upcoming annual GirlDefined Conference. We threw out a number of ideas and just couldn't seem to land on the right topic. The discussion continued for several months and we were still coming up shorthanded. We decided to commit some intentional time to praying for the upcoming conference and asking God for wisdom. After a few weeks of prayer, the two of us met again. God had clearly worked through our prayers. We both came back with the exact same idea—*radical purity.* That was it! We were going to have a conference on God's amazing and radical design for sexuality and purity.

The months that followed were packed with planning sessions and organizing details. As the conference drew closer, I (Bethany) remember feeling a bit intimidated by the theme. The idea of digging into the nitty-gritty details of sexuality and purity and speaking about it at a conference wasn't exactly something I was excited to do. I wondered how the young women would respond when Kristen and I brought up words such as *porn*, *masturbation*, and *lust*. Would they be uneasy? Would they feel uncomfortable? Would they get mad at us for having a conference on such personal issues? Would they even come back after the opening session? To be totally honest, the thought of hundreds of women gathering to hear us talk about sexuality, lust, and purity kind of freaked me out. I was fearful about what these young women might think about the two of us. I knew we had prayed about the topic, but it was still scary.

To make matters even worse, I began to imagine what might happen after we finished the opening session. I envisioned looking out into the audience and seeing hundreds of women staring up at the two of us in horror with shocked faces and wind-blasted hair. I know it sounds crazy, but that's really what I had pictured.

When the GirlDefined Conference finally arrived, Kristen and I stood backstage before the opening session and prayed. We prayed for God's wisdom. We prayed for all the attendees. We prayed God would do a mighty work in our hearts and in the hearts of every woman in attendance. As the two of us walked out onto the stage and stared into the faces of so many precious young women, we realized how needed the message truly was. In that moment, we felt privileged to bring such crucial truth into their lives.

The young women who attended the conference that year were more receptive than we could have ever anticipated. They were open and honest about some of their deepest and most private struggles. They willingly confessed their secret addictions and battles with lust. They sought extra counsel from our prayer team and recommitted their lives to the Lord. The weekend was nothing short of inspiring. They proved to us, and to themselves, that women genuinely want victory through the power of Christ.

I'm glad to report that these girls didn't look up at us in horror with shocked faces or wind-blasted hair. Instead, they had the opposite reaction. They were excited and hungry to talk openly about God's truth regarding their sexual design.

Changing the narrative about lust will be hugely helpful for Christian women. With more people talking about lust as a *human problem* (not just a guy problem), our hope is that more women will be honest about their struggles. As sexually broken women, we're all in this together. We're all in need of help, encouragement, and hope.

Women genuinely want victory through the power of Christ.

As you think about the problem of lust and the status of our society today, you may easily get discouraged. Sexuality may feel more like a curse than a blessing. Everywhere you turn you come face-to-face with alluring temptations inviting you to join in. Has the world always been this way? Has sexuality always been this broken? Understanding how things got so distorted is crucial to learning how to fight the battle of lust biblically.

3. WHEN EVERYTHING RIGHT WENT WRONG

The two of us love animals. We always have. In recent years, our love for animals compelled each of us to get a dog of our own. White, fluffy Maltipoos to be exact. We both adore our dogs beyond what's normal. If you visited us on a workday, you'd find two six-foot-tall blondes sitting at a table working on our computers with a Maltipoo in each of our laps.

As much as we love our dogs and think they're perfect, there is one downside to owning them. Grooming. Since they're non-shedding dogs, their hair has to be manually trimmed every few months. This gets expensive. Fast.

Not too long ago, I (Kristen) was getting really tired of forking over the cash every time my dog, Sadie, needed a haircut. As cute as my dog looked after each visit, she was killing my budget. So, I did what any normal dog-loving, budget-conscious owner would do—I took matters into my own hands. I had some experience with giving my husband, Zack, haircuts, so how hard could it be to cut a dog's hair? If I could learn how to cut Sadie's hair, then I could spend that money on something fun. Like new house decorations. Or maybe a pedicure. Or I could get my own hair done.

After watching a few tutorials online, I couldn't believe how easy it was going to be. *I've been paying how much for that?! You've got to be kidding me.*

This was going to be a piece of cake.

To start things off, I set Sadie up on top of a large box so I could trim her hair from different angles. Since the professionals in the videos used electric trimmers, I decided to do the same. Zack had a nice electric trimmer set on hand, and I figured he wouldn't mind sharing it with the dog.

Everything was going great, until I turned on the trimmers. Without warning, Sadie jumped off the box and ran out of sight. The trimmers apparently terrified her. After what seemed like an hour, I finally got her to sit still on my makeshift hair-cutting table. But the minute those trimmers went on again, she tried to bolt. By the third time, I was ready for it. Holding her down with one hand, I kept her in place. Then, with my other hand, I started running the trimmers through her hair. She squirmed. She moved. She tried to jump. I got even smarter. After piling a delicious array of treats in front of her nose, she finally sat still. For three minutes. She was not having it.

After three long hours, I was dripping with sweat, exhausted, and more traumatized than the dog. Finally finished, I turned off the trimmers and collapsed into a chair. Sadie jumped down in relief. When I called her over to me to admire my handiwork, I couldn't believe my eyes. Somehow, in the midst of the battle, I lost sight of the bigger picture. Instead of cutting her hair evenly and in the "Maltipoo fashion," I did the opposite. Not sure whether to laugh or cry, I stared down at my haircut disaster. Rather than looking like her cute self, she looked more like an oversized hamster that had been run over by a lawn mower. She looked awful—and nothing like her original self. In fact, it was hard to even recognize her. She was the same dog but a very distorted version of her.

Too embarrassed to leave her in that chopped-up state, I had only one choice. *The groomer's.* Suddenly, forking over the cash sounded very affordable. A bargain, in fact! With Sadie in tow, I shamefully drove three miles to the groomer's. As I walked in, I could see the groomer's eyes light up in shock. Then, without saying a word, she took Sadie in her arms and smiled at me. "We'll see you in an hour," she said with a wink.

She was the same dog but a very distorted version of her.

Sadie was saved from my disastrous haircut.

As funny as Sadie's haircut situation is to think back on, the thing that sticks in my memory the most is how different she looked from her original self. Her haircut was so bad, you couldn't even tell she was a Maltipoo anymore. She looked nothing like her original design.

As I think about the current state of sexuality today, I realize it's in a similar condition to Sadie's haircut. Sexuality has been so chopped up, reshaped, and altered that it looks very different from what God originally designed it to be. We, as humankind, have strayed so far from God's original purpose and intent for our sexuality that most of us have accepted the chopped-up version as normal. Without the original design in view, we no longer know what's right. We no longer know what's good. Sex is no longer linked to marriage. Truth is no longer linked to God. As a result, we're pursuing a myriad of personal choices regarding our sexuality without a compass guiding us to true north. The way we navigate our sexuality today is similar to someone trying to put together an extremely complex puzzle without the photo on the box to guide them.

As we step back and survey the landscape of sexuality today, we don't see a beautiful masterpiece. Rather, we see a vast sea of confusion, pain, and hurt. Taking the reins from the One who designed us didn't make things better. Instead, it magnified the depth of our brokenness.

As you look around at the brokenness surrounding sexuality (in society and in your own life), have you ever wondered how we got here? When did it go so wrong? When did things become so confusing? Why are we all struggling so much? Has it always been this way?

Thankfully, as chopped up as things may be today, it wasn't always this way—and it won't be this way forever. There was once a time when sexuality was perfectly beautiful. Perfectly understood. Perfectly enjoyed. Perfectly embraced. In fact, it was paradise. Once upon a time real humans walked on this earth, thriving in their flawless sexuality. Their sexual desires were in perfect harmony with the Creator's intent. But clearly, something went wrong. Let's travel together back in time to this exotic and mysterious place. The place where our sexual design was first created.

There was once a time when sexuality was perfectly beautiful.

Sexual by Design

With the sun shining brightly in the sky, day six of the world's existence was well underway. God had created everything except one thing—humankind. Unlike the animals, trees, and atmosphere, this final creation would be the pinnacle of God's work. The humans would be uniquely designed to reflect the image of God Himself. "Then God said, 'Let us make man in our image, after our likeness'" (Gen. 1:26). More than anything in all creation, humankind would tell the story of the One who created them. Their special design would mirror their Designer.

With great intentionality and purpose, God handcrafted the first human from the dust of the earth (see Gen. 2:7). God designed the first human to be *male* (see Gen. 2:7). He was a full-grown man with male anatomy, male hormones, and a male reproductive system (see Gen. 1:28). God wove a sexual design into the very fabric of his being.

Even in those early moments of creation, the man's physical sexual design mysteriously hinted at something more. His physical body was clearly designed *for* someone else. But who? No other human was on the earth.

God had a plan.

God put the man in the Garden and assigned him the task of naming all the animals. It became very clear that all the animals had counterparts, but there wasn't a "helper fit for him" (Gen. 2:20). God then put the man into a deep sleep, took a rib from his side, closed the wound, and began forming a brand-new creature (see v. 21). With great care and precision, God handcrafted the second human to be unique. She was *female*. She was distinctly different from the male. As a full-grown woman, she had female anatomy, female hormones, and a female reproductive system (see Gen. 1:28). Her sexual design as a female also spoke of something more. Her body was uniquely designed to *receive* someone.

As Adam rubbed his sleepy eyes awake, he looked up to see the most breathtaking creature. *She* was made *for him*. With great excitement, he jumped up and proclaimed,

> This at last is bone of my bones
> and flesh of my flesh;
> she shall be called Woman,
> because she was taken out of Man. (Gen. 2:23)

God brought the woman to the man and blessed them both. He then said, "Be fruitful and multiply and fill the earth and subdue it" (Gen. 1:28).

Unlike animals, which were created with sexual instincts, humans were created for sexual *intimacy*. They were created for in-depth bonding with one another. They were created to share a deeply emotional and satisfying relationship with one another. They were made to enjoy exclusive sex as a pleasurable bond within their lifelong relationship.

At this time, God established a specific structure for this new relationship—marriage. This is the first time we see glimpses of God's plan for the covenant marriage. "Therefore a man shall leave his father and his mother and hold fast to his *wife*, and they shall become one flesh" (Gen. 2:24, italics added).

In the perfect Garden, the first couple embraced God's design with great joy and delight. Standing there, in the middle of paradise, they were naked and were not ashamed (see v. 25). He was fully male. She was fully female. They were both fully sexual. In the beauty of the Garden, they enjoyed the pleasures of sexual intimacy with total freedom, complete trust, and abundant joy. They felt no pain. No reservations. No shame. No confusion. The first husband and wife took great delight in God's good and beautiful design for their sexuality.

> *Unlike animals, which were created with sexual instincts, humans were created for sexual intimacy.*

40

Because the story of Adam and Eve has become so familiar, it is easy to brush over the details. But when we pause and look a little closer, we see profound truths. We see God's intentional design in making us male and female. Nothing was shameful or embarrassing about our sexual design. We see God's beautiful plan for sexual intimacy, created within the context of the marriage relationship. Sex was a passionate celebration between husband and wife. We see God's purposeful act in creating two distinct genders. And in all this, we see God at the center of everything as he created humans to be His image bearers.

However, as beautiful as the story of Adam and Eve is at this point, God was up to something even bigger. In all these details, He was laying the groundwork for a much greater story. A story that would teach the world about Himself and who He is. Genesis doesn't reveal what it means when God used plural words about Himself—"Let *us* make man in *our* image" (Gen. 1:26, italics added)—but as we'll discover in chapter 6, God had an intentional plan for all these things. Since the Bible is one continuous story about God from beginning to end, we have to keep reading to get the bigger picture.

But for now, we can marvel at the fact that our Creator is extremely purposeful in *everything* He does.

When Everything Right Went Wrong

While the first humans were enjoying life in perfect harmony, a dark shadow was making its way into the Garden. Something evil was brewing. The Bible says the serpent (Satan) "was more crafty than any other beast of the field that the LORD God had made" (Gen. 3:1). This dark creature hated God and was on a mission to destroy His creation. And since the male and the female were created specifically to reflect

God's own image, they were the perfect targets. If this dark enemy could deceive the humans, he could destroy their lives and distort the image they bore.

The serpent chose to target the woman with a deceptive question: "Did God actually say, 'You shall not eat of any tree in the garden'?" (v. 1).

She responded, "We may eat of the fruit of the trees in the garden, but God said, 'You shall not eat of the fruit of the tree that is in the midst of the garden, neither shall you touch it, lest you die'" (vv. 2–3).

The serpent went on to tell the woman she wouldn't actually die, but she would become like God. If she ate the fruit, she would know good from evil. Her eyes would be opened to new and exciting things. She would be enlightened (see vv. 4–5).

The woman listened. She pondered. She believed.

What the serpent said sounded good to her. With her husband standing silently by her side (see v. 6), she made a decision that would drastically alter the world forever. After she bit into that delicious, juicy fruit, her life would never be the same again. She handed some to her husband and he ate it too. Suddenly, everything changed. The Bible says, "Then the eyes of both were opened, and they knew that they were naked. And they sewed fig leaves together and made themselves loincloths" (v. 7).

For the first time, sin entered the lives of Adam and Eve. They suddenly felt things they never had before. Shame. Guilt. Confusion. Regret. Hurt. Betrayal.

Sin would forever mar the perfect life they had shared together. Their flawless sexual relationship would forever be broken. Their desires and longings would forever be self-gratifying. But worst of all, their perfect relationship with God, their Creator, would forever be hindered.

For the first time, God's perfect design for humanity took on a pale and chopped-up version of its original self.

Wandering Eyes, Questioning Hearts

Can you imagine how shocking those first few moments must have been for Adam and Eve? Don't you wonder what was going through their minds the moment sin flooded their existence? Did they talk about it? Did they regret every moment from that point on? The fatal scene with the serpent probably played over and over in Adam's and Eve's minds. *What were we thinking? Why did we listen to him? Why didn't we trust God?*

The male and the female were experiencing brokenness for the first time.

From that point on, every human who entered the world arrived broken. As the days, months, years, and centuries stretched on, each generation experienced its own sexual struggles as a result of sin. Adam's and Eve's original decisions to reject God's truth was the beginning of a worldwide domino effect. What God had created to be beautiful and perfect had been greatly distorted.

Sin now pollutes our desires and feelings. Galatians describes these warped desires as being contrary to what is right and true: "For the desires of the flesh are against the Spirit, and the desires of the Spirit are against the flesh" (5:17).

The male and the female were experiencing brokenness for the first time.

We can trace the brokenness and chaos we see today back to that fateful moment in the Garden. The moment when everything right went wrong. The sexual pain and confusion we each face today are a direct result of Adam's and Eve's initial sins. We can easily cast judgment on Adam and Eve, but the truth is, we're a lot more like them than we realize. They went wrong in the same way most of us still go wrong today. Rather than trusting in God and looking to Him for guidance, they turned their eyes away from Him. They fixed their gaze on something else. As their eyes wandered, their hearts questioned. *Did God really say? Is He really good? Can we really trust Him?* With their eyes wandering and their hearts questioning, they believed the great deceiver (see 2 Cor. 11:3).

Our struggles are no different from Eve's. We're tempted to question God's truth on a regular basis. *Did God really say I should reserve sex for marriage? If I love someone, does anything else really matter? If I feel a certain way, wouldn't God want me to be true to my feelings? If pornography doesn't seem to hurt anyone, it should be fine, right? As long as I don't go all the way, I'm not technically breaking any rules. God wants me to enjoy sexual fulfillment, so He's probably okay with me reading erotica. Did God actually say it's wrong to have sexual fantasies?* Our eyes wander and our hearts question—just as Eve's did. Did God really say? Doing things our own way seems better in the moment. We're tempted to believe the age-old lie that we know better than God.

We're tempted to believe the age-old lie that we know better than God.

Regardless of what era, country, or society we look at, sexual chaos *always* follows the rejection of God as Creator. The more a society moves away from God, the more convoluted and distorted sexuality becomes within that society. This is exactly what's happening in our society today. Rather than defining sexuality on God's terms, we're defining it according to our terms. As a result, the ways in which sexuality is often embraced, expressed, and pursued today are a far cry from what God originally designed it to be.

4. FOUR CULTURAL LIES ABOUT OUR SEXUAL DESIGN

Several years ago, the two of us had the opportunity to spend a few weeks in the beautiful country of Austria. If you ever have the opportunity to go to Austria, you need to visit the little town of Saalfelden. It's gorgeous! We might be a little partial to that city in particular because our Nana was born and raised there. Imagine how much fun the two of us had traveling to Saalfelden and staying in the house our Nana grew up in. It was a dream come true.

Although we wished the trip could have lasted forever, it didn't. The time flew by, and it felt as though we were heading back to Texas as quickly as we had left. The trip back home is never quite as exciting as the trip to the anticipated destination. Our particular trip back home from Saalfelden was an extra drag. The travel was painfully long due to a twenty-four-hour layover in Florida. On the way to the US, I (Bethany) ended up in one of the worst seats on the plane. I was squished in the middle seat, in the middle row, in the very middle of the plane. As if that wasn't bad enough, the seats surrounding me were occupied by two men who never needed to use the restroom.

I'm serious. We flew for ten hours straight and I don't think they got up once. I, however, am pretty much known as the queen of the small bladder. I'm sure those two men were so annoyed by my constant in and out to use the restroom. Oh well. A girl's gotta do what a girl's gotta do.

Anyway, I sat in my seat and tried to sleep, which felt impossible. I tossed and turned and got all sorts of pains in my neck and back. Let's just say it was one uncomfortable flight. At about the five-hour traveling mark, the guy on the right side of me awoke from his slumber and decided to pass the time with a little entertainment. He scrolled through a few of the available options and landed on his movie of choice. If you've ever been on an overseas flight and ended up sitting in the middlest of middle seats, as I did, you know how easy it is to see everything around you. It's honestly hard *not* to be in everyone's business. Even when I was looking straight ahead, doing my own thing, I could still clearly see the guy's screen out of the corner of my eye. I tried to ignore the movie he was watching, but it was hard to avoid. What happened next completely caught me off guard. The scenes that began to play on his screen were surprising, to say the least. Keep in mind that this was a very full and very long overseas flight on a public airplane with families traveling on it. Children were in the rows behind me and young teens were sitting in the rows to the right and left of me.

What happened next completely caught me off guard.

Suddenly, without warning, the actors and actresses on the screen began stripping down and jumping into bed with one another. I glanced at the guy next to me to see if he was fazed by the explicit scene playing on his screen. He didn't seem a bit concerned. In fact, he looked a little bored. For

46

the next hour or so, the little screen on the back of that airplane seat was filled with nudity and sex scenes, publicly displayed for all to see.

Even though I tried to avoid looking at the screen, I still caught a few glimpses. I saw stuff. Stuff I wish I hadn't seen. Stuff that God created to be shared between a husband and wife in the privacy of their own sacred marriage. Stuff that should be beautiful and respected. Stuff that should be cherished.

One scene in particular seared itself into my brain. Not because it was so hot and steamy but because of the opposite. Instead of being super sexy, the scene appeared casual and cheap. There was nothing special about what the couple was doing. Nothing sacred. Nothing private. The two people seemed to be going through the motions for a little bit of pleasure.

To top everything off, the guy watching the movie fell asleep. Like, dead asleep—with snoring and all! Not even sex on a screen was interesting enough to keep this guy awake.

We've Come a Long Way

When the two of us think about the way society portrays sex, we feel pretty disheartened. Sex is literally everywhere. It's used to sell everything. Think about it. Sex is used to sell everything from alcohol to makeup to music to movies to prom dresses to big and tough trucks. Sex has infiltrated every aspect of society. In fact, one of our younger sisters recently got a sample mascara tube with bold letters that read "Better than Sex." If mascara is "better than sex," then we might as well forget about sex altogether and just go slap on a few more coats of mascara.

That's clearly not the answer though.

We live in a society that has made sex easily accessible to everyone. It has become as common as a handshake. If you want to have sex, you can have it almost instantly. With a quick swipe or a click, you can find a partner to hook up with within miles of your location. If you want to watch other people have sex, you can access porn within seconds. Instant viewing pleasure is available to all. If you want to read about sex, you can download an erotic novel the moment you wish. Sex has become so commonplace that it often feels cheap, meaningless, and as if it's no big deal.

Sex has become so commonplace that it often feels cheap, meaningless, and as if it's no big deal.

When I (Bethany) think about that guy on the airplane, I feel as though his reaction is the perfect portrayal of how society views sex—it's so common that it will put you to sleep.

Instead of being proud of how sexually liberated we've become as a society, we should stop for a minute to really think about where we are and whether this is where we want to be. Do we like the idea of sex being tasteless, casual, accessible, and void of lasting commitment and intimacy? Do we like the idea of a hookup culture? Do we like the idea of two individuals using each other for selfish gain? Do we like the idea of marriage being completely redefined? If we'd stop for just a second and seriously think about how most people treat sex, we'd probably be pretty disappointed.

In their book, *Pulling Back the Shades*, Dr. Juli Slattery and Dannah Gresh describe our societal changes this way: "Our society's moral relativism isn't a sign of advancement but is the result of foolishness and pride."[1] Society prides itself on what it sees as sexual advancement. It relishes the

48

fact that we're liberated from old ways of thinking and free to be what we want to be. When you stop and think about it though, what have we really advanced from? What are we so proud of? Are we proud that the porn industry is worth a whopping $97 billion globally?[2] Are we excited that a child's first exposure to porn is typically around eleven years old?[3] Are we patting ourselves on the back because the average girl loses her virginity at seventeen years old?[4] These are statistics not to celebrate but to be saddened by.

The sexual advancement we see in society today has only moved us further and further away from the Creator's good design for sexuality and intimacy. We've declared ourselves the new experts, leaving the Designer in the dust.

EXPOSING THE LIES ABOUT OUR SEXUAL DESIGN

Sex and sexuality are two of the hottest topics in society right now. With so many voices expressing opinions, it can be confusing to know what's truth and what's not. What did God actually say about our sexuality in comparison to what we're seeing happen in our society? If we, as Christian women, are not vigilant to discern the lies from the truths, we will end up listening to whichever voice is shouting the loudest.

When we choose to embrace anything but God's good and original design for our sexuality, we buy into an inaccurate reflection of who God created us to be. We accept a false version of our truest identity. That's why the two of us want to unpack a few of the biggest lies permeating society today. Our goal is to expose the lies and work toward getting back to who God originally created us to be.

Keep in mind that this chapter will focus exclusively on the lies. We have several more chapters coming up that will unpack God's truth and really dig into His amazing plan for our sexual design.

Lie #1: Sexual Identity Is Determined by Personal Desires

When the two of us met Lisa, she was struggling to understand her sexual identity. She had dozens of questions and couldn't seem to find solid answers. Over the past few years, she'd been dealing with same-sex attraction and had no idea how to handle her desires. She wondered, *Should I suppress my desires or should I let them flourish?* Lisa was very much at a loss for answers. She'd grown up attending church and was familiar with God's design for male and female relationships but was confused because she felt attracted to women.

Lisa would often lie in bed at night and ponder what her high school counselor had told her during their sessions. "It's your body, your sexuality, and your brain. You can choose to act on your desires in whatever way feels right to you! Don't let anyone tell you what to do or not to do. Be true to your inner self." The counselor had also given Lisa some pamphlets to take home as a way to help her process her thoughts. Inside the pamphlets, Lisa read things like this:

> Sexual orientation is about who you're attracted to and want to have relationships with. Sexual orientations include gay, lesbian, straight, bisexual, and asexual. Sexual orientation is different from gender and gender identity. Sexual orientation is about who you're attracted to and who you feel drawn to romantically, emotionally, and sexually. It's different than gender identity. Gender identity isn't about who you're attracted to, but about who you *are*—male, female, genderqueer, etc. Sexual orientation is a natural part of who you are—it's not a choice. Your sexual orientation can change over your lifetime.[5]

50

After reading statements like these, Lisa was even more confused. *Why is this all so complicated?*

Lisa felt restless and very much alone in this journey.

When she first approached the two of us, she seemed hesitant about sharing what was on her heart. Opening up and talking about her inner struggle with same-sex attraction was a big deal for her. It takes a lot of courage to be vulnerable about such personal matters. Lisa showed bravery in taking this step and doing what so many of us are often too afraid to do. She chose to be honest about what was going on in her heart, and we were humbled that she was willing to share it with us.

After talking for fifteen minutes, Lisa started to share even more. She told us that her biggest fear in being honest about her struggle with same-sex attraction was the condemnation and disapproval from other Christians. She was sure we (along with other Christian women) would be ashamed of her struggles and send her away as a lost cause. She genuinely wondered if the Bible had anything helpful to say about sexual identity. Did God care about her sexuality? Was His design for gender even applicable for her? Could she trust God with this sensitive area of her life?

> She genuinely wondered if the Bible had anything helpful to say about sexual identity.

Our short time with Lisa turned out to be so much more than either of us could have hoped for. We started out with handshakes and introductions and ended with heartfelt prayers and genuine hugs. We didn't have all the answers for Lisa, but she walked away with a new sense of confidence in God's love for her and a renewed hope in exploring the Bible for answers. Opening up about her inner struggles was a huge first step for Lisa in her journey toward truth, resolutions, and freedom.

Lisa is not alone in her search for answers. In an article titled "The Clarity of Complementarity: Gender Dysphoria in Biblical Perspective," the question is posed, "Does the church of Jesus Christ have anything unique, anything distinctive, anything worth saying in the modern conversation over gender dysphoria?"[6]

The topics of sexuality, sexual orientation, and gender identity are overwhelmingly prominent in our modern society. From our schools to our workplaces to our entertainment to our friends and family, everyone has an opinion on these topics. On one hand, society tells us each person must follow their own heart and be true to their inner desires. We're directed to be genuine and authentic to who we feel we are. According to society, there is no higher authority, and every person is left to realize their orientation and discern their truest identity on their own. On the other hand, the Church tells us our orientation and identity should be informed by God's Word. We're advised that there is a higher authority and God's Word should inform our desires and inner thoughts regarding our personal identity. Sadly, that's often where the conversation with most Christians ends. There isn't much follow-up, and few one-on-one conversations and discipleship relationships take place. Those of us within the Church who are struggling with our sexual identity often have a lot of questions and can't seem to find many in-depth answers. This needs to change.

As the two of us have seen the complexities grow larger and the questions increase each year in regard to sexual orientation and gender identity, we believe these issues are too big to leave to human knowledge alone. They're too big for society to answer. They're too complex for even doctors and psychologists to fully figure out. We're all in need of better answers. We need answers that have a proven long-term track record. We need answers that won't change in ten, twenty, or fifty years.

We need answers that have a proven long-term track record.

What we truly need is to understand the heart of God and His deep love for each and every one of us regarding our identity. We need to understand the why behind His creation of humanity as a whole and His purpose in creating gender. We need to get to know the heart of the God who created this entire world and everyone in it. He has something to say about our sexuality. He cares deeply for each one of us and has a beautiful plan for our lives.

Lie #2: Marriage Is a Union between Any Two Partners

In doing research for this book, the two of us googled the definition of marriage. The top hit was from the good old faithful *Merriam-Webster's Dictionary.* Here's how it defines marriage: "The state of being united as spouses in a consensual and contractual relationship recognized by law."[7] We noticed that the definition omits any male or female pronouns. The description was intentionally written to be very gender-neutral. As we continued scrolling down the page, we saw that *Merriam-Webster's* also includes a caveat to its definition. It says, "The definition of marriage shown here is intentionally broad enough to encompass the different types of marriage that are currently recognized in varying cultures, places, religions, and systems of law."[8]

In addition to *Merriam-Webster's* current definition, here's how a popular psychology magazine describes marriage:

"Marriage is the process by which two people make their relationship public, official, and permanent. It is the joining of two people in a bond that putatively lasts until death, but in practice is increasingly cut short by divorce."[9] Just like *Merriam-Webster's*, this magazine avoids using pronouns that would limit marriage to a man and a woman. It also emphasizes that marriage is increasingly being cut short by divorce. Not decreasingly but increasingly. Marriage isn't getting better and better, it's getting worse and worse.

After reading both these modern descriptions, we decided to also look up the word *marriage* in the 1828 edition of the same dictionary to see if it was defined differently. The contrast was shocking. Here's how it describes marriage: "The act of uniting a man and woman for life; wedlock; the legal union of a man and woman for life. Marriage is a contract both civil and religious, by which the parties engage to live together in mutual affection and fidelity, till death shall separate them. Marriage was instituted by God himself for the purpose of preventing the promiscuous intercourse of the sexes, for promoting domestic felicity, and for securing the maintenance and education of children."[10]

What a drastically different description.

When comparing both dictionary definitions side by side, it's clear that *Merriam-Webster's* has completely rewritten their original definition of marriage to reflect the ever-evolving and changing views of people in today's society. Marriage is no longer defined as being between one man and one woman, instituted by God. It's an open entity for anyone who desires to live life with another person. *Merriam-Webster's* chose to conform to society's modern version of marriage to be relevant and viewed as a reliable source of information. If they didn't, they would be disregarded for their narrow-minded and old-fashioned beliefs.

The pressure to conform to modern views of marriage isn't just hitting *Merriam-Webster's*; it's hitting each one of us. The issues we're discussing throughout this book are hard to talk about because of the ever-growing societal pressure to conform. They're also hard to navigate because of the way they affect many of us in extremely personal ways. It's hard to decide what's true and what's not. It's hard to know when to take a stand and when to be quiet. It's hard to embrace biblical truth in a world that isn't open to God's Word. It's hard to be viewed by society as outdated and old-fashioned.

The two of us are right there with you in all this. But just because it's hard doesn't mean we should give up on truth.

We, as Christian women, need to be strong and diligent in chasing down truth. Even though it's counter-cultural, we need to get back to what the Creator intended marriage to be. He designed it and therefore is the only One with the authority to define it. His original design for marriage truly is for our own good.

> *We need to get back to what the Creator intended marriage to be.*

Lie #3: Sex Should Be Embraced in Whatever Way Seems Right

Jennifer grew up in a Christian home and was actively involved in church. She went to youth group, participated in the church choir, and even volunteered on Sunday mornings with the kids' class. When Jennifer graduated from high school and left for college, her family had high hopes for her. They felt certain she would remain committed to her moral upbringing and stand strong through the college years.

Year one of college went great for Jennifer. She made close friends, earned good grades, and seemed to be doing well. Year two came around and that's when trouble started to surface. Jennifer began to feel a little insecure about her moral standards and convictions. It seemed as though everyone on campus was talking about their latest sexual escapades. Fastforward to year three and Jennifer began hanging out with a new group of friends. This group just so happened to include one really nice and very handsome college guy named Jake. Slowly but surely Jake noticed Jennifer and began paying her some extra special attention. After many months of being just friends, the two of them started a romantic relationship. And that's when the pressure began.

Jennifer's new group of college friends began asking her about the sexual side of her relationship with Jake. They seemed confused as to why she wasn't having sex with her boyfriend. They would say things such as, "Don't the two of you love each other?" "Sex is simply a physical expression of how much you and Jake care for each other." "You need to stop overthinking this." "Everyone is doing it. It's normal." The constant pressure eventually got to Jennifer. The compromise was slow—three years in the works—but it was still there. She slowly lost sight of God's intended design for sex and intimacy. She took her eyes off His bigger purpose and began listening to the voices around her instead. One night after Jennifer and Jake went out on a date, he asked her to have sex with him. She said yes. Jennifer decided that her passionate feelings toward Jake were worth following.

We, as modern women, live in a culture much like Jennifer's college world. The messages are similar. "If it feels right, just go for it!" "If you love him, it's okay to sleep with him." "If you want to have sex, don't hold back." "Everyone is doing it, so don't overthink it!" "Just follow your heart."

I (Kristen) recently read an article from a 2016 issue of *Teen Vogue* aimed at helping teen girls decide if they are ready to have sex for the first time. Here's a bit of what the article has to say:

> More than anything, though, you want to feel *ready*. But what does that mean? We turned to 7 experts for their insight on the subject to help guide you through. Herein, all they had to say. . . . Having the right partner is key. . . . Know what makes you feel good. . . . Have sex because *you* want to. . . . If you can't talk about STDs, you're not ready. . . . Make sure both you *and* your partner are comfortable and ready. . . . If you're grossed out by bodily fluids, you're not ready. . . . You should never feel pressured. . . . Having sexual desire is important.[11]

The article goes into detail on each of these eight points, but I won't drag you through it. In summary, the article says there is no standard of truth when it comes to sex. Feelings are the best guide. If it feels right, do it. If you feel ready, do it. If you're "in love," go for it. According to *Teen Vogue*, feelings are the driving force in determining when it's the right time to start having sex. The idea of marriage is obsolete and self-restraint isn't much of a thing. That's basically the crux of what the entire article has to say.

Sex can't be minimized and reduced to two people enjoying a passionate exchange. Sex is about so much more than feelings and doing what seems right in the moment. It's so much more than a bodily action between two consenting people. God has a much bigger purpose and design for sex that we all desperately need to understand.

Sex is an amazing and life-giving gift from God. Although it sounds good to say "I can act on my sexual desires in whatever way feels good," this view is shallow and shortsighted.

It has no substance. Where is the purpose? The direction? The meaning? The *why* behind sex? Sex is too beautiful, too intimate, and too passionate to be left up to our own discretion. We need guidance from the Creator of sex to embrace it in all its glory.

Lie #4: Femininity Is about Being Seductive and Powerful

Several years ago, I (Bethany) had the opportunity to sit across the desk from a high-ranking modeling agency owner. I'd been recruited by this agency multiple times and finally decided to give them a try (you can check out the full story in our book *Girl Defined*).

As Jeff, the owner of the agency, and I talked, it became very apparent that he had a specific goal in mind for all his models. He explained to me that I needed to be willing to pose nude if I wanted to climb the modeling ladder. That's what he expected from his models and that's what he expected from me. He wasn't interested in anyone trying to hold his agency back. He wanted success and knew just how to get it.

The moment I hinted to Jeff about my disinterest in stripping nude for the camera, a look of shock flashed across his face. He literally spent the next several minutes lecturing me about my moral standards. He told me I was insecure for holding onto such old-fashioned ideas. He looked directly in my eyes and scolded me for not being comfortable in my own skin. Jeff made it very clear I was not welcomed back until I was ready to do whatever it took to be a successful model.

My interview with Jeff confirmed what I'd been seeing and hearing in society. Women are only as powerful and valuable as their outward appearance. If we're hot and willing to show off our bodies, we will go places. If we're not willing, we won't go places. Women with sexual morals and values are often considered insecure and prudish.

Sadly, this is the position many of us, as Christian women, find ourselves in.

If a woman can strike a sexy pose, take a super hot photo, and come across as totally enticing, she's often propped up like a trophy. But decency, modesty, and a heart toward purity are considered negative qualities we should bury and burn. We hear messages such as "Real women are willing to show off their bodies." "Strong women know how to use what they've got." "Sexy women know how to make a man crazy about her." It takes only one glance at a magazine rack in a checkout lane to confirm that being seductive and provocative are the qualities to embrace if you want to be a powerful woman.

Whether or not we, as modern women, are willing to admit it, the essence of femininity has been reduced merely to a woman's outward appearance. Although society portrays women in a hypersexualized way, femininity is about so much more than that. It's about more than looking hot, gaining power, and having men notice you. It's more than having your body plastered on the front of a magazine. It's more than being called a "queen" or a "goddess."

God designed women for so much more than seduction and power.

God designed women for so much more than seduction and power. He doesn't measure our worth the same way society does. He has a beautiful plan for our womanhood that far surpasses the often-degrading values of our culture.

Girl, This Is Complicated

This chapter was not an easy one to write, and we're guessing it was not an easy one to read. Over the past few years as we've studied and researched sexuality and had face-to-face conversations with women just like you, the two of us have realized just how complicated these issues have become. Everything discussed in this chapter points to the pain, brokenness, and confusion surrounding sexuality. The pain and confusion so many of us have personally experienced.

Think about the cheapness of sex. Think about the brokenness of marriage. Think about how complicated gender and identity have become. Think about the way women are often objectified. This is not what God originally designed our sexuality to look like.

God created us for so much more than the confusion and chaos we see today. If we, as women, want to experience God's good and intended design for our sexuality, we need His help. We need His rescuing. We can't climb out of this mess on our own. We need Him to redeem us from our brokenness.

Part two

God's Spectacular Design

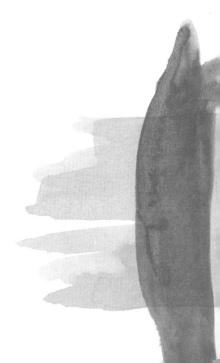

5. THE HERO EVERY WOMAN NEEDS

We both (Kristen and Bethany) sat with our eyes glued to the screen. The drama unfolding before us was captivating. We could feel the turmoil as the desperate situation played out in the movie. The people were in serious trouble and needed someone to rescue them. As we watched, all hope seemed lost.

Just as darkness was ready to claim victory, something changed. The wind shifted. Someone was coming.

Without warning, the hero showed up on the scene. This courageous rescuer made short work of the evil and saved the people from the clutches of darkness. With shouts of joy and gladness, the people rejoiced. They were saved.

Drama. Struggle. Rescue. Victory. Whether it's reenacted on the screen or happening in real life, there's just something captivating about a rescue mission. New books and movies regularly capture audiences with these same dramas. As humans, we all seem to share a common interest in watching these types of stories unfold.

Have you ever wondered why we're so drawn to the struggler-saved-by-hero narratives? Maybe it's because something deep inside of us personally resonates with the struggler. Maybe we can relate to what it's like to feel hopeless and lost. To secretly long for someone to save us. This is true for the two of us, and we're guessing it's true for you as well. As tough as we may look on the outside, deep down we long for someone bigger and stronger to be our protection and guide. When it comes to our sexual struggles, this is especially true. We long for someone to save us from the pain and shame we carry. We long to be redeemed from our sexual brokenness. We want someone to swoop in and rescue us.

As we've interacted with hundreds of women over the past few years, we've heard this longing in their voices too.

The desire to be rescued isn't new—it's an age-old longing. It's something humanity has been craving from the beginning of time. As we saw in chapter 3, the very first story of brokenness and struggle took place in the perfect Garden, when everything right went wrong. As Adam and Eve hid themselves from God in shame (see Gen. 3:8), they knew they couldn't fix the problem. As sin flooded their lives and polluted their sexuality, they knew they were in serious trouble. They needed someone bigger and stronger to help them. They needed a hero.

We long for someone to save us from the pain and shame we carry.

Just as Adam and Eve needed a hero then, we too need a hero today. We need someone to forgive us of our sin and guilt. We need someone to redeem and restore our sexuality. Our inner longings for a hero constantly remind us that we aren't enough. We can't fix what has been broken. We desperately need a *Savior*.

Rescuing Sexuality

Over the years, the two of us have been guilty of trying to cover and hide our sexual brokenness. We didn't want to face it. We didn't want others to see it. Whether it was lust, sexual fantasies, masturbation, or something else—we were too ashamed to stare our sin straight in the face. Instead, we tried to mask it with temporary fixes. We wore our gold-star-Christian-girl faces and pretended everything was just fine. Sure, it worked for a little while. But it never lasted.

I (Kristen) remember a specific time during my teen years when I was really struggling with lustful fantasies. I would sit in my room and get lost in my thoughts, daydreaming about sexual experiences with certain guys. As embarrassed as I am to admit this now, I would even kiss the wall in my room, pretending it was a hot guy.

Every time my mind wandered into those lustful places, I would feel really guilty and promise never to do it again. But no matter how hard I tried, I would find myself in that same place of sin and lust again. I wanted to be strong enough, but I could never do it long term. Here's where I went wrong. Instead of acknowledging my need for a hero, I was trying to be the hero. And that's why I wasn't experiencing long-term change. In and of myself, I wasn't strong enough to conquer the sin in my heart.

Trying to be our own hero must be a common reaction to sin, because that's exactly what happened with Adam and Eve after they sinned for the first time. Remember the evil serpent and the juicy fruit? Shortly following their devastating choice, the Bible says Adam and Eve immediately tried to cover their nakedness with fig leaves (see Gen. 3:7). They were trying to mask the problem. As God watched them cover their nakedness, He knew they would need more. They would need not only a more substantial covering for their bodies but also a more substantial covering for their sin.

Verse 21 says, "And the Lord God made for Adam and for his wife garments of skins and clothed them." God stepped in to help them cover their sin. The fig leaves weren't sufficient. This verse reveals that an innocent animal had to die because of Adam's and Eve's decisions. To us, as modern women, killing an animal might seem like a strange provision from God, but it was actually a profoundly important and symbolic act. In killing the animal to make their clothing, innocent blood was shed to cover the shame of another. By doing this, God was showing Adam and Eve that sin is costly. It requires a great sacrifice. It requires more than what they were able to contribute. In this messy and bloody moment, this first sacrifice was actually foreshadowing the ultimate sacrifice that would one day take place through Jesus Christ (see John 3:16). Jesus would be the ultimate sacrifice and covering for sin.

Although Adam and Eve didn't understand the greater implications happening here, God was setting into motion His ultimate rescue mission. By these small and intentional acts, He was forecasting His bigger plan to redeem humanity from the power of sin, evil, and brokenness.

As Genesis concludes and the rest of the Old Testament unfolds, we're left with the hope of a Savior to come. Fast-forward a few hundred years, and the New Testament begins. Something good was about to happen.

The wind had shifted. *Someone was coming.*

Entering the Fray

The New Testament begins with a picture of the courageous hero hinted to in the Old Testament. The perfect Rescuer was making His way into our broken world to destroy the power of sin. Coming in the form of an everyday man, God himself entered the fray of humanity. He came to save the world from the very sin Adam and Eve brought into the Garden. He came to offer hope and freedom in the midst of our sexual brokenness.

God, in the form of Jesus Christ, entered our dirty, damaged, and messed-up world to show us how much He loves us. He healed the blind (see Mark 8:22–25). He fed the poor (see Luke 9:10–17). He touched the untouchable (see Luke 17:11–19). He loved the unlovable (see Luke 7:36–50). As the rescue mission unfolds throughout the four Gospels (Matthew, Mark, Luke, and John), everything seems to be heading toward the climax of the story.

After living a perfect life for thirty-three years on this earth, Jesus knew it was time. The purpose for His mission had come.

The costly price of sin would be met with the gracious sacrifice of the Savior (see Rom. 5:8).

Jesus was ready and willing to take the punishment humankind rightly deserved. He was ready to die in our place by taking our guilt and sin on Himself. He was willing to sacrifice His own body to satisfy the just and righteous wrath of God. With his hands and feet nailed to a cross, Jesus bore the weight of the world's sins—including our sexual sins—on His shoulders (see 1 John 2:2). Every lustful thought. Every glance at porn. Every indulgence in sexual fantasies. Every immoral relationship. All of it. Jesus died in our place so we could be forgiven.

Jesus died in our place so we could be forgiven.

As Jesus hung on the cross—bloody, bruised, and beaten— hope must have seemed lost to those believers watching at that moment. As He breathed his last breath and collapsed unconscious, they must have thought the story was over. The hero of the world was dead.

For three dark days, Jesus lay in a tomb.

Darkness was winning.

Just as the Evil One was ready to claim victory, the ground began to shake (see Matt. 27:51). The large stone in front of the tomb miraculously rolled away. Then Jesus did something that shocked the entire world.

He rose from the dead.

Jesus is alive!

He broke the power of death and conquered sin once and for all (see 1 Pet. 3:18). "O death, where is your victory? O death, where is your sting?" (1 Cor. 15:55). Through Jesus's death and resurrection, He absorbed all our guilt—past, present, and future. He paid the punishment for all our deepest, darkest, and most shameful sexual sins. He died for the sin we try to cover and hide. He died and provided the true covering we all need. Because of Jesus, we don't have to hide behind fig leaves anymore. We can accept the perfect covering of forgiveness and righteousness He gives us. As John Piper says, "God came into history in Jesus Christ. He died in order to destroy the power of hell and death and Satan and sin, and he did it through the gospel of Jesus Christ."[1] Jesus died so we could be free. Matthew 20:28 says, "The Son of Man came . . . to give his life as a ransom for many."

The hero was victorious. The rescue mission was successful.

Jesus did what He came to do. Our inner longings for a hero have been fulfilled in Jesus Christ. He is the One our soul yearns for.

Instead of trying to be our own hero, we can now bring our sin, guilt, and shame before Jesus in humility and He will receive us. We don't have to be enough, because Jesus was enough for us. In fact, there's no point in even pretending to be enough, because God sees the reality of our hearts. He sees our sin more clearly than we even see it. That's why He graciously sent Jesus to die for us. He knew we needed rescuing before we even realized it. There is now hope and freedom in being honest about our sexual burdens and confessing them to God in prayer. Jesus Himself said, "I came that they may have life and have it abundantly" (John 10:10). Because of Jesus's death and resurrection, we have the power to conquer every sexual sin and struggle. We have the power in Him to resist sexual temptation.

Deep down, in the hidden places of sexual shame and brokenness that you carry, Jesus offers freedom. He offers forgiveness. He offers restoration. He offers new life. If you place your faith in Him as your Savior and accept His sacrifice on your behalf, you will gain eternal life (see John 3:16). You will also gain access to a personal relationship with God Himself.

We don't have to be enough, because Jesus was enough for us.

Once you accept Jesus as your Savior, the Bible says you are made new! You are given a source of power and strength you didn't have before. Instead of you continuing to hopelessly drown in your sin, you are called out of your old ways and into a new life with Him. The apostle Paul describes this incredible transformation in the book of Galatians:

> I have been crucified with Christ. It is no longer I who live, but Christ who lives in me. And the life I now live in the flesh

I live by faith in the Son of God, who loved me and gave himself for me. (2:20)

As believers who are made new in Christ, we're now enabled to view our "old selves" as dead to the power of sin. Even though we can't escape our sinful bodies on this earth, we're called to walk in faith by looking to Christ for our strength.

She Was Made New

A woman named Kate has a powerful testimony of how Jesus transformed her "old self" and made her new in Him. As a young woman, Kate was obsessed with romance novels and did whatever it took to get guys to notice her. She gave her body away to multiple boyfriends, hoping it would be enough to keep them. It never was. As the years stretched on, she knew her life was heading in a downward spiral. Erotica, porn, and numerous other lustful pleasures became her constant companions. As a Christian woman, she knew her sexual choices weren't honoring to God, but she wasn't sure how to adjust her course. She tried changing her actions many times, but the change never lasted. Nothing seemed to work.

Then one day she reached a breaking point.

She was exhausted and weary of trying to be her own hero. She was tired of the endless promises to change. Although she looked fine on the outside, she was desperately broken and hurting on the inside.

One night, she found herself sobbing on her bedroom floor. Pouring her heart out to God, she confessed her pride of trying to live life on her own. She confessed her sexual sin to God and repented of her rebellious choices. She asked for

God's forgiveness and prayed for His transforming grace to give her a heart of purity.

That night marked a turning point in Kate's life. Instead of living life in her own strength and for her own pleasures, she now looked to Christ to transform her heart. She was no longer chasing after the fleeting pleasures of this world but was instead seeking to find total satisfaction and fulfillment in her relationship with Jesus. Her journey toward freedom wasn't without bumps and rough patches, but the more she deepened her relationship with Christ, the more her desires and longings changed. She found a mentor from her church and did whatever it took to stay accountable.

She now looked to Christ to transform her heart.

As the years stretched on, Kate's life looked nothing like it had before. Her old self was gone. She was a free woman. Jesus broke the chains of habitual sin in her life and empowered her to walk in the freedom of God's transforming grace.

Kate's life is a beautiful example of Jesus's transforming power. Regardless of what you're struggling with right now, there is hope for your future. Like Kate and the two of us, Jesus can transform your heart and sexual brokenness as well.

What went terribly wrong in the Garden, Jesus came to make right. Jesus is the true hero every one of us desperately needs. He came to break the bondage of sin in our lives and to set the captives free (see Ps. 107:13–16; Luke 4:18).

We don't have to live as slaves to our sin any longer. We don't have to bear the weight of our sexual brokenness and shame anymore. We don't have to listen to the enemy's lies. We don't have to buy into the world's counterfeit version of sex. We don't have to crumble under the weight of our own guilt. We have been given new life in Jesus. We have been set free. We have been made new. And through Jesus Christ, we are now empowered and called to walk in that freedom.

6. FOUR BIBLICAL TRUTHS ABOUT OUR SEXUAL DESIGN

As teen girls, the two of us loved playing basketball. Our competitive natures served us well on the court. We won a lot of games. Victory tasted oh so sweet. It also helped that we had an amazing coach (our dad) and are both over six feet tall. We enjoyed not only playing basketball but also watching it. Being from the great state of Texas and the even greater city of San Antonio, we grew up watching our local NBA team. When we were younger, we especially admired one particular player on the team. He was tall (7'1") and athletic, and he played the same position that we did on the court. In our minds, he was the epitome of epicness. Yes, *epicness*. If you know your NBA history, you might remember him—good ol' David Robinson (aka The Admiral). As much as we admired his basketball skills, we were even more impressed with his outspoken life as a Christian.

One time during a conference in San Antonio, we had the opportunity to hear him speak. David, who stood head and shoulders above everyone else, leaned down onto the podium and shared transparently from his heart. He talked about the challenges of embracing his faith in a world of professional sports and endless temptations. He expressed how important God was to him and how much he valued his wife and children. His goal was to honor God in everything he did—whether on the court, at home, or on the road away from his family. His courageous stance on sexual purity and marital faithfulness gained national attention. The public took notice.

In 1996, *Sports Illustrated* did a cover feature of him titled "Trials of David." In the story, Robinson describes how he handled himself, as a professing Christian, husband, and father, in the midst of the NBA's intense temptations. For example, during television breaks, he would sit on the bench and stare studiously at the floor to avoid looking at the gyrating cheerleaders out on the court. The article also mentions that like all NBA players, Robinson was constantly approached by attractive women who wanted to talk to him . . . and were probably offering more than just witty conversation. Apparently, he would rather brusquely brush them off. When asked to comment on that seemingly "rude" practice, he said something like this: "If any woman is going to get her feelings hurt, it's not going to be my wife."[1]

In a world of casual sex and one-night stands, the media took note of this man who passionately cherished his marriage. David valued the commitment he had made to his wife more than a cheap thrill. He cherished the sacredness of the marriage bed and sought to honor that covenant. Onlookers often scratched their heads in amazement, but David was only doing what he knew was right. His conviction was rooted in his personal relationship with his Savior, which he exemplified in the way he lived. David Robinson wasn't just an NBA player—he was a Christian man living for the glory of his King.

The two of us were inspired by David as teen girls, and we're still inspired by him today. He believed the Word of God and embraced it wholeheartedly in his life. He wasn't swayed by pop culture or the spotlight of fame. He didn't adopt popular ideas just because everyone else did. He looked to God's Word to inform his worldview about love, sex, and marriage. He built his life on truth.

David Robinson wasn't just an NBA player — he was a Christian man living for the glory of his King.

As Christian women today, we can learn a lot from this basketball veteran. He didn't settle for short-lived sexual thrills, and we don't have to either.

As C. S. Lewis so famously said, "We are half-hearted creatures, fooling about with drink and sex and ambition when infinite joy is offered us, like an ignorant child who wants to go on making mud pies in a slum because he cannot imagine what is meant by the offer of a holiday at the sea. We are far too easily pleased."[2] What God has to offer us is a thousand times better than the watered-down pleasures of society. His design for sex, marriage, and womanhood is stunningly beautiful. He is *for* these things and wants to show us how to embrace them rightly. When we take God at His word and put our trust in His plan, we will experience true freedom as never before. Will it be easy? No way. It wasn't easy for David Robinson. And it won't be for you. But the fight is undoubtedly worth it. God's ways are always better.

It's time to leave the dirty mud pies behind and chase after something much more compelling.

WHICH GIRL WILL YOU BE?

Before we dig into the details of God's good design for sexuality, we need to first stop and decide where our truth is going to come from. Before we can have a conversation about sex, we need to have a conversation about God. A lot of voices offer conflicting messages about sex, marriage, and identity, so who are we going to listen to? Will we turn to God for answers or will we listen to the popular voices of society? Will we listen to our own feelings and opinions or will we research what the Bible teaches?

As you live your life right now, you can't help but come face-to-face with dozens of hot-button questions. Is sex before marriage wrong? What about porn? What's your opinion on gay marriage? Do you think living together before marriage is a sin?

Before we can have a conversation about sex, we need to have a conversation about God.

If you had to answer each of these questions right now, what would you say? And more importantly, where would your answers come from? As Christian women, we have to decide what's going to be our source of truth. Will we choose to embrace all of God's Word or only the culturally acceptable passages? Will we allow the Bible to shape our worldview or will we allow our worldview to shape the Bible?

As you seek to answer these tough questions, you will automatically default to one of three categories: (1) the girl who denies all of God's Word, (2) the girl who cherry-picks God's Word, or (3) the girl who accepts all of God's Word. Whether or not you realize it, one of these will be your default.

Here's a closer look at what each of these girls looks like.

1. Denier Girl

This girl rejects God's Word entirely and denies anything it has to say about sex and her sexuality. When it comes to her sexual design, she prefers to live by her own rules. She's a follow-your-heart kind of girl who makes decisions that feel good in the moment.

2. Cherry–Picker Girl

This girl doesn't fully reject God's Word, but she doesn't fully accept it either. She's kind of stuck in the middle when it comes to her faith. She wants to do the right thing, but it's just too hard sometimes. Societal pressures often get to her and she ignores the Bible when it conflicts with what's easier to believe. She definitely claims to be a Christian, but she totally cherry-picks what she wants to believe from the Bible.

3. Accepter Girl

This girl genuinely believes God is her Designer and allows the Bible to define her beliefs. She chooses to totally live by the truth, even when it's hard and even when she doesn't feel like it. She trusts that God's design for sex and her sexuality is a good thing and she believes His ways are for her best. The Bible is her foundation of truth and she filters every decision and belief through His Word.

When it comes to the myriad of perspectives about sexuality permeating society today, you need to decide which kind of woman you're going to be. Will you choose to be *Denier Girl*, who rejects God's Word; *Cherry-Picker Girl*, who accepts some of what the Bible has to say and rejects other parts of it; or *Accepter Girl*, who takes God at His Word and truly embraces everything He has to say?

Our prayer for you is that you will choose to be *Accepter Girl*. That you will build your worldview on the solid foundation of God's timeless truth (see Ps. 19:7–11).

Opinions come and go. Cultures change over time. Feelings ebb and flow. But the Word of God is constant. "The grass withers, the flower fades, but the word of our God will stand forever" (Isa. 40:8). May we be a generation of Bible-believing women who stake our confidence in the solid rock of God's unchanging Word.

EMBRACING THE TRUTHS ABOUT OUR SEXUAL DESIGN

In chapter 4, we unpacked four cultural lies about our sexual design. Now, we're going to counter those lies with God's compelling truths. Understanding who God created us to be is crucial for answering some of life's toughest questions. Without a biblical foundation for your beliefs on issues such as gender, sex, marriage, and femininity, it's easy to be swayed by personal desires and popular opinions.

Regardless of where you've been or what you're currently wrestling with, our prayer is that you will find comfort and hope in God's good design. John 8:32 says, "And you will know the truth, and the truth will set you free." God's truth brings freedom. Lean into that and embrace it. You were created to be a beautiful reflection of your Creator. And your sexual design is a spectacular part of that.

Truth #1: Sexual Identity Is a God-Assigned Reality

Jackie Hill Perry is a woman who experienced same-sex attraction for the first time when she was five years old. Nobody taught her how to like girls . . . it just happened. These feelings were part of her life for as long as she could remember. As she grew into a teenager, the feelings only intensified. By age seventeen, she pursued her first female relationship and openly embraced her life as a lesbian.

Then, at age nineteen, something radical happened in her life. She was introduced to a man named Jesus. She had never known a love so powerful before. She had never known a God so intimate. Over the next few years, Jesus transformed her life from the inside out.

Perry shares her journey of finding her true identity in Christ in her book, *Gay Girl, Good God*. When she took her brokenness and pain to the foot of the cross, Jesus lovingly and radically transformed her entire life. The more she grew in her relationship with Jesus and in understanding His greater plan for her womanhood, the more her heart was softened by His truth. Over time, her identity was no longer defined by her desires. Instead, it was defined by her new role as a daughter of the Most High King. Now, her greatest passion is to live her life for God's glory.

If you're wrestling with conflicting feelings about your sexual identity or know someone who is, we want you to know you're not alone. We know it can be extremely painful and confusing. It can often feel like a lonely and isolated journey. But, sister, God sees you and He knows you. He loves you deeply. He wants nothing more than to draw you into the beautiful freedom of His transforming grace. As you wrestle, know that you're not wrestling alone. Lean into God's truth and He will meet you right where you're at.

As Jackie Hill Perry came face-to-face with the gospel, she was confronted with a challenging and personal question. Who has the authority to decide one's identity? Is it me, or is it God? In an article titled "Genitalia Are Not Destiny—But Are They Design?" John Piper poses these questions: "Is gender set by a preference of the individual, or a providence of God? Or to put it another way: Is my sex determined by my decision in my mind, or by God's design in my nature?"[3]

When we look to society to answer these hot-button questions, we're passionately told to fulfill our own desires. We're told to "follow our hearts" and "be true to ourselves." Christopher Asmus, a pastor who has a testimony similar to Jackie Hill Perry's, says, "The overarching sexual ethic of our day is 'I feel, therefore I am.'"[4] Human autonomy reigns supreme. Although this sounds somewhat compelling and freeing, it leaves no room for God. This ideology actually leads us to find our identity in our sexual desires rather than in Christ. Our feelings and inner longings become the gods in our lives. As a result, we end up labeling ourselves with identities God never gave to us.

Feelings and desires can be tricky things though, no doubt. Going against something that feels so right can often seem counterintuitive. Jackie Hill Perry shares her own struggle of wrestling with her inner sexual desires. As she grew in her understanding of God's truth, she learned to view her feelings and desires from a biblical framework and discovered they weren't as true and good as she had thought.

Going against something that feels so right can often seem counterintuitive.

When sin entered the world, it polluted and distorted our inner desires. As a result of sin, the natural inclination of our hearts became warped and bent away from God. That's why toddlers don't have to be taught how to whine, throw fits, and hit their siblings. These things come naturally to them. The Bible describes these distorted desires as being contrary and opposed to what is right and true. As we've seen previously, "For the desires of the flesh are against the Spirit, and the desires of the Spirit are against the flesh" (Gal. 5:17). Christopher Asmus puts it this way: "As a result of the fall, our hearts are out of order and dark (Romans 1:21). Instead of loving light and hating darkness, we love darkness and hate light (John 3:19). And as we fall more in love with darkness, we sin and choose the way of death (James 1:14–15; Proverbs 14:12)."[5]

When we view our sexual desires from a biblical framework, it becomes clear that following our hearts isn't a wise choice. Apart from Christ, our hearts aren't going to lead us toward truth, righteousness, or freedom. In fact, "The heart is deceitful above all things" (Jer. 17:9). Our hearts are actively deceiving us; therefore, we should be wary of staking our entire identity on the basis of how we feel.

As we learn to view our desires from a biblical framework, we must understand another key element: sinful desires don't have to define our identity. Since our feelings and desires have been distorted by our indwelling sin nature, each one of us will face unwanted sinful temptations on a regular basis. We all wrestle with this broken reality every day. As challenging as this is, let's not make the mistake of labeling our sexual identity according to our sinful desires. If we are Christians, our identity is made new by who we are in Christ (see 2 Cor. 5:17). We are sinners redeemed and forgiven by Christ. We are defined not by our sin but by the blood-bought identity of becoming a Child of God. Thanks be to Christ, we now have the power to respond righteously to sinful desires and temptations. When a sinful desire surfaces in our hearts (whether a same-sex desire or heterosexual desire), we can act in one of two ways: we can either respond in the flesh and indulge in the sinful desire or we can respond righteously by the power of the Spirit and resist indulging in the sinful desire. We need to revisit Romans 8:5–13 often to remember that victory is found in Christ as we choose to walk in the Spirit:

> For those who live according to the flesh set their minds on the things of the flesh, but those who live according to the Spirit set their minds on the things of the Spirit. For to set the mind on the flesh is death, but to set the mind on the Spirit is life and peace. For the mind that is set on the flesh is hostile to God, for it does not submit to God's law; indeed, it cannot. Those who are in the flesh cannot please God.
>
> You, however, are not in the flesh but in the Spirit, if in fact the Spirit of God dwells in you. Anyone who does not

have the Spirit of Christ does not belong to him. But if Christ is in you, although the body is dead because of sin, the Spirit is life because of righteousness.

As strong as our sexual desires may be at times, we have the power of Christ living within us to empower us to respond righteously. Our sexual identity does not have to be determined by our sinful desires or temptations. Rosaria Butterfield is another woman who has a powerful story of how the gospel transformed her life and freed her from homosexual desires. She says, "There is a world(view) of difference between saying that you struggle with same-sex sexual attraction and that you are gay. One allows you to stand apart from your struggle, seeing homosexuality as a part of the Fall; the other collapses your identity into your struggle, seeing sexual orientation as a morally neutral reality."⁶

Jesus Christ came to this earth and died on the cross so that we could be freed from the power of sin in our lives. In Him and through His strength, we're no longer slaves to sin but slaves to righteousness (see Rom. 6:17–18). In Christ, we have not only the power to resist temptation but also the ability to grow and change from who we were to who Christ calls us to be.

Jackie Hill Perry found that discovering these biblical truths was both liberating and conflicting. As her flesh waged war on her spirit, she turned to prayer:

> As I was praying and meditating on [God's truth], God put this impression on my heart: "Jackie, you have to believe that my word is true even if it contradicts how you feel." Wow! This is right. Either I trust in his word or I trust my own feelings. Either I look to him for the pleasure my soul craves or I search for it in lesser things. Either I walk in obedience to what he says or I reject his truth as if it were a lie.⁷

Jackie discovered that instead of embracing her inner desires as truth, she must turn to God's timeless and unchanging Word to guide her toward truth. Psalm 119:105 says, "Your word is a lamp to my feet and a light to my path." God's Word is like a lamp in our lives, lighting the path of truth for us to walk in. The road ahead wasn't easy for Jackie. It was full of ups and downs, bumps and struggles. In an interview with *Christianity Today*," she shares the following:

> As a former lesbian . . . I had a particular challenge when it came to learning how to embody womanhood the way it is described in the Scriptures. I also had to learn how to discern whether people teaching about womanhood were using God's version or culture's version. I saw how people were putting their culture into the texts instead of allowing the text to shape their culture.
>
> So for me, it was a lot of hard work to get back to the basics of what God has to say. When I started to actually see my womanhood through the lens of Jesus, it was really helpful. Bending my womanhood to what I see in Jesus changes everything.[8]

Jackie Hill Perry, Rosaria Butterfield, and many other women have discovered the life-changing freedom of allowing God to define their sexuality and womanhood. As they've submitted their desires to Him, their lives have been radically transformed by the power of the gospel. Their identity is no longer found in who they think they are but in who Christ has created them to be.

As countercultural as this reality may be, our truest self can only be found within the Creator's design for us. He designed us; therefore, He is the only One who can define us. As John Piper says, "Neither whom we should worship nor who we are sexually is left to our preferences."⁹ God created you to be a female. He chose your gender for you. Your sexual identity is a beautiful, God-assigned reality. May we, as Christian women, lean into that truth and strive to embrace His design for our womanhood. May we pray for humility and obedience as we seek to be authentic image bearers whose lives tell the true story about our Creator.

Your sexual identity is a beautiful, God-assigned reality.

Truth #2: Marriage Is a Covenant between a Man and a Woman

With hundreds of eyes watching us, I (Kristen) stood on the platform across from my soon-to-be husband, Zack. With his hands grasping mine, I felt the weight of this moment. This wasn't an ordinary day. This was a huge deal. With my heart beating faster in excited anticipation, I said my wedding vows to Zack. In front of hundreds of witnesses, I expressed my commitment to be married to this one man until "death do us part." Zack spoke the same vows to me. As the pastor pronounced us husband and wife, an invisible covenant bound us together in a lifelong union. Regardless of what the future would bring, we were making a promise to stay faithful to each other, no matter what.

In our society today, marriage can mean a million different things to a million different people. Depending on who you're talking to, you could get a myriad of descriptions and definitions. As we saw in previous chapters, modern society has taken the position that marriage is nothing more than a contract between two people with the goal of finding personal happiness. Many people believe marriage is simply a man-made institution designed to keep people civilized. If that's the case, then "a human-made institution can always be expanded or reformed to accommodate the wishes of humanity."[10]

But what if that isn't the case? What if our inner longings for companionship, intimacy, sex, and procreation aren't just man-made ideas? What if they are part of a God-ordained design?

As Christian women who are striving to be faithful to God's Word, we have to approach marriage with these foundational questions: Who created marriage? Why was it created? How should it be rightly embraced?

As we discussed earlier in this book, God first set marriage into motion when He united Adam and Eve as husband and wife (see Gen. 1:28; 2:24; Mark 10:6–9). At this point, we see that God's design for marriage has wonderful benefits, such as mutual comfort, companionship, offspring, and sexual fulfillment. It's not until we read the New Testament that we see God has a bigger purpose for marriage. As we put the pieces together from Genesis to Revelation, we uncover an incredible and glorious masterpiece. From the beginning of time, God intentionally created marriage to tell the redemptive and beautiful story of the gospel.

In our book *Love Defined*, we explain this a little more in-depth:

> Marriage, as lovely as it is, is only a picture of something greater. It's an earthly representation of something much grander. God placed the institution of marriage on the wall of this world as a representation of the gospel. "Therefore a man shall leave his father and mother and hold fast to his wife, and the two shall become one flesh. This mystery is profound, and I am saying that it refers to Christ and the church" (Eph. 5:31–32).
>
> God's greatest purpose for creating marriage is to show the world an earthly representation of what Christ's covenant

relationship looks like with His Church. Christ is the groom and the Church is His bride.[11]

Unlike a contractual agreement, the marriage relationship is patterned after God's own covenant relationship with His people, the Church. A covenant is a promise so strong and binding that it cannot be broken. God created marriage as a way to show the world what His covenant love and faithfulness look like for His children. The male/groom is a reflection of Christ and the female/bride is a reflection of the Church (see Eph. 5:22–24). Author Tim Challies writes, "Marriage is not a man-made institution primarily for man's benefit, but rather a God-made institution primarily for God's glory."[12]

A covenant is a promise so strong and binding that it cannot be broken.

Defining marriage according to God's terms is crucially important for displaying an accurate picture of who God is and what the gospel means. When two people of the same gender unite together and call it marriage, the union fails to tell the true story of Christ and His Church. When a couple decides to live together instead of getting married, it fails to tell the true story of God's covenant love. When a marriage is riveted with adultery and divorce, it fails to tell the true story of God's faithfulness and promise.

Our greatest aim as Christian women should be to glorify God in everything we do. This includes the way we embrace and define marriage.

Truth #3: Sex Was Created for Intimacy within Marriage

In a society that portrays sex as an endless buffet of unlimited pleasure, we're often led to believe that unrestrained sexual activity is always better. But before we blindly jump on board with these popular messages, we need to dig a little deeper. We need to ask some pointed questions. Is premarital sex *always* better? Is unrestricted sexual activity truly fulfilling? Do one-night stands actually fill the ache in our heart?

In doing research for this book, we came across an online forum where someone posted the question, "Is sex completely boring to anyone else?" In response, one person commented, "I don't know about anyone else, but I have lost complete interest in sex. I've seen it all and done it all. You could even say I'm 'oversexed.' I find it to be a boring chore nowadays and I really see no point in doing it anymore."[13] Many other people in the forum felt the same way. With access to unlimited sexual opportunities and experiences, boredom was the outcome.

God created sex to be so much more than ecstasy and momentary pleasure.

Pastor Garrett Kell writes, "The world portrays pleasure as flash-in-the-pan passion that moves from lover to lover and fantasy to fantasy. But does this sort of pleasure really fulfill? Or does it actually deepen our discontentment? Who clicks on one pornographic picture and stops, satisfied? Who fantasizes for a few seconds and stops, satisfied? The offering of worldly pleasure can't satisfy a heart that was created for a deeper, lasting pleasure."[14]

God created sex to be so much more than ecstasy and momentary pleasure. Just as God was intentional with every other aspect of our human design, he was intentional with sex too.

Dr. Juli Slattery offers the following mind-blowing insights into God's bigger plan and purpose for sex:

Of all the things God has created on earth to teach us about His character, none is more powerful in creation or pervasive in Scripture than the marital covenant and the place of sexuality in it. Why is sexuality so important to God. . . . Because sexuality is a holy metaphor of a God who invites us into covenant with Himself. God created you as a sexual person in order to unlock the mystery of knowing an invisible God. . . . God created male and female—our bodies, emotions, and desires—to teach us about covenant love.[15]

God has woven into the very fabric of our being a deep desire and longing to be intimately satisfied within a covenant relationship. Just as God created marriage to be a metaphor of Christ's relationship with His Church, sex was created to be an earthly metaphor of Christ's covenant love with His Church. There is no other act on this earth as intimate, vulnerable, and close as sexual intimacy. This physical act reveals a glimpse of how deeply God loves His people.

When God created Adam and Eve, He created them *for* marriage and *for* covenant (see Gen. 2:24; Heb. 13:4). Inside of the marriage covenant, He then gave them sex as a way to celebrate their covenant love. God designed sex to be a physical celebration of the love, commitment, and vulnerability we share within marriage. According to Dr. Slattery, "Sex within marriage is like a sacrament. It's doing with our bodies something physical to remind us of the covenant promise that we make to one another."[16]

Sex is not only a beautiful celebration of the marriage covenant but also a way to deepen the bond between a husband and a wife. Dr. Slattery says, "When you look at what happens in our bodies and brains when you're sexually intimate with someone, you're actually bonding with that person in ways that you don't understand—even at a neurological level."[17]

We were made for covenant. We were made for committed love. That's how God loves us, and that's how He designed a man and a woman to love each other within a covenant marriage. Sex outside of marriage completely falls short. There is no covenant. Without marriage, the intimate act of sharing your body with another person is a false celebration. Tim Keller notes that "sex is supposed to be a sign of what you [have] done with your whole life, and that's why sex outside of marriage, according to the Bible, lacks integrity. You're asking someone to do with your body what you're not doing with your life."[18]

Even prior to marriage, our sexual desires are reminders that we were made for an intimate relationship. "While God created sexual desire to awaken our longing for love, even marriage is not the ultimate fulfillment of that desire," writes Dr. Slattery. "Marriage is the shadow, the foretaste, the metaphor of the true longing to be known, embraced, accepted, and celebrated by our Creator."[19] Regardless of whether you're single or married, you were made for real intimacy with Jesus. Ultimate fulfillment can be found only in a covenant relationship with the Savior. No amount of earthly sex can satisfy our inner ache for a deep relationship with God. The psalmist writes,

Regardless of whether you're single or married, you were made for real intimacy with Jesus.

> As a deer pants for flowing streams,
>   so pants my soul for you, O God.
> My soul thirsts for God,
>   for the living God. (Ps. 42:1–2)

Sex is a spectacular gift given to us in marriage as a picture of God's love. May we be women who steward this gift wisely, cherish it highly, and enjoy it *authentically*.

Truth #4: Femininity Is a Display of God's Design for Womanhood

As we talked about in chapter 3, femininity is often portrayed as power and confidence in a woman's physical beauty and sexual expression. This is a tricky issue because it's mixed with partial truths. The female body *is* beautiful. A woman's sensuality *is* intoxicating. God created us with the ability to be powerfully alluring and enticing. As Dannah Gresh describes it, "Female beauty is a powerful force. Advertising gurus have discovered that if you put the photo of a woman in an ad, you can increase the length of time someone spends looking at it by as much as 30%! It doesn't quite work that way when you use a photo of a man."[20]

Feminine allure and sensuality are actually part of God's good and original design for us. The desire to be enticing and feel attractive is a core aspect of our womanhood. We, as women, long to be desirable. We want to be sexy. God created us to be wildly enticing . . . but not for just anybody. Our sensuality was created to be a private gift for the marriage bed. When feminine allure is used to fan the flame of intimacy within marriage, it's an awesome thing.

Gresh writes, "Proverbs 5:18–19 reads 'May your fountain be blessed and may you rejoice in the wife of your youth. A loving doe, a graceful deer—may her breasts satisfy you always, may you be ever intoxicated by her love.' That's a steamy verse. A more literal version of the last phrase might be, 'may you be intoxicated by her sexuality.' The female body is powerfully tempting and tantalizing and in the context of marriage this is a wonderful thing."[21]

The problem isn't that we, as women, are powerfully intoxicating and beautiful—it's that we often use our beauty and femininity in ways that aren't honoring to God. We can use them for selfish gain (power, immorality, manipulation, personal gratification, etc.) or we can embrace them in ways that bless others and glorify God.

Proverbs 9 includes a powerful illustration of "wisdom and folly" displayed through the narrative of two women who use their feminine influence in very different ways.

First, we see a picture of femininity portrayed as "wisdom." This woman loves her family and always has their best interest in mind (see vv. 1–2). She doesn't go along with what's popular but rather courageously calls others to a higher standard (see vv. 4–6). She loves wise counsel and seeks it out. She is eager to grow in wisdom and truth (see v. 9). She understands that the fear of God is essential to being a wise woman (see v. 10). She is focused on the big picture and wants to live a life she won't regret (see vv. 11–12).

Next, in contrast to this wise woman, we see a picture of "folly" displayed in a woman who is "seductive and knows nothing" (v. 13). She uses her feminine allure and beautiful body to sexually entice men who aren't her husband (see v. 13). She longs for the attention of men and is constantly on the hunt for it (see v. 14). She loves being naughty and convinces herself that sin is actually fulfilling (see v. 17). She is blind to the sin in her life and can't see the deadly path she is going down (see v. 18).

Biblical femininity is beautiful, strong, intelligent, and compelling.

God desires for us to embrace our femininity with wisdom and discretion. He wants us to use our beauty, influence, sexuality, and intellect in ways that bless others and advance His kingdom purposes. Our value and worth don't come from our physical looks, sex appeal, accomplishments, or how much attention we get from men; they come from our Creator (see Ps. 139:13–14).

Biblical femininity is beautiful, strong, intelligent, and compelling. We're worth far more than the objectification this world has to offer us. We have been given immense dignity and worth because of our Creator. May we express our femininity in ways that reflect our true identity as daughters of the King and glorify the One who redeemed us. To learn more about biblical womanhood, we encourage you to grab a copy of our book *Girl Defined.*

Embracing God's Good Design in a Confusing World

In a world of confusing messages and ever-evolving definitions regarding sexuality, marriage, intimacy, and femininity, God's Word is constant. His design for our sexual identity, which He established at the beginning of creation, has never changed. His plan for marriage has been the same since He designed it. His purposes for sexual passion and intimacy have always been set within the context of marriage. He's always intended for our femininity to be a beautiful expression of our womanhood. God's context and concept for all these things are good and right.

We know we've covered a lot . . . and you don't have to figure out everything right now. God is simply calling you to take that first step of trust. He is calling you to be a woman who wholeheartedly embraces His truth.

7. GIRL, YOU WERE MADE FOR INTIMACY

I (Bethany) was trying my best to act cool and collected. I sat on the edge of my couch and just waited. *He said he'd call at seven. Just relax.* I tried to calm myself down. But I couldn't. This was a big deal for me, and I was really looking forward to it. As a single woman in my midtwenties, a phone call with a serious suitor was exciting. Like, really exciting. For all I knew, he could be the one . . . the one I'd been dreaming of my entire life. My prince. My man.

Ring. Ring. Ring.

The sound of the phone interrupted my thoughts. I jumped off the couch and hurried to grab my phone. This was it. Landon was calling.

The conversation started out so smoothly. We chatted about our days, discussed the latest happenings in our lives, and just had such a blast talking on the phone to each other. I anticipated getting to know him even better. The two of us had met a few months before that and totally hit things off. Unfortunately, we didn't live in the same city, which complicated the relationship process. If you've ever done long-distance dating, you know how difficult it can be. It requires a lot of phone calls, video chats, emails, and even a little bit of snail mail. Thankfully, both Landon and I felt committed to getting to know each other. If that meant phone calls, we were up for it. We wanted to make this relationship work. At least, I thought we both did.

Landon and I continued to talk. The days turned into weeks and the weeks eventually turned into months. However, as time went on, I began to notice an uneasy feeling in my heart. Although Landon and I were talking on a regular basis, something wasn't right. Our conversations were long, but that was about it. There was no depth to them. We were talking, but we weren't growing any closer. We weren't really getting to know each other. Yeah, we knew facts about each other, but our hearts were very much at a distance. Instead of feeling excited about Landon's calls, I started to dread them. I didn't want to spend another three hours on the phone simply chitchatting.

My heart craved something deeper.

It wasn't long before the relationship ended. And to be totally honest, I was relieved when it did. I desired something more than what Landon and I had shared. My heart craved something deeper. Something more meaningful. Something more intimate. If God had marriage in my future, I wanted to truly know my husband's heart and for him to truly know mine. I didn't want the relationship to be shallow.

God Wants to Know You

We, as women, live in a day and age when shallow relationships abound. Dating relationships, marriages, friendships, and even family relationships often stay on a surface level. Despite that many of us crave to know and be known on a deeper level, we may find it extremely difficult to actually attain that level of intimacy. We want to go deeper, but we're often afraid or unsure of exactly how to make that happen. Sadly, many women (single and married) spend their entire lives feeling the pain of loneliness. Their hearts long for true love and true friendship, but they don't know what to do or how to get these things.

Over the past few years, the two of us have discovered the meaning and importance of these longings. The desire to experience true intimacy isn't accidental. It's not something we, as women, should shove aside or strive to satisfy in temporal ways. The desire to be truly known and truly loved is actually at the very core of who God created us to be. As our Father, God longs to know each one of us on a personal level. He wants to have a deep and meaningful relationship with each of us.

In fact, God uses a very specific Hebrew word throughout the Bible to help us understand his intimate love for us. The word is *yada*.

In Hebrew, the word *yada* literally means to know deeply or intimately. "The word *yada* appears in the Old Testament more than 940 times. . . . The word *yada* is most often used to describe intimacy with God—His with us, and ours with Him."[1] God intentionally uses the word *yada* to help us *He wants to have a deep and meaningful relationship with each of us.*

see that He doesn't want a casual or surface-level relationship. That's not why He created us. He wants to yada us and for us to yada Him back. He created us to know Him and to have a deep and satisfying relationship with Him.

As the two of us looked at some of the more than 940 uses of yada in the Old Testament, we found that we were familiar with many of the verses. Although we'd read many of the passages multiple times throughout our lives, we'd never fully understood their true meanings. It wasn't until we learned exactly what the Hebrew word *yada* meant that we more fully grasped the depth of God's love for us.

Look at the context for how *yada* is used in these verses:

O LORD, YOU HAVE SEARCHED ME AND KNOWN [YADA]
    ME. . .
FOR YOU FORMED MY INWARD PARTS;
    YOU KNITTED ME TOGETHER IN MY MOTHER'S WOMB.
I PRAISE YOU, FOR I AM FEARFULLY AND WONDERFULLY
    MADE.
WONDERFUL ARE YOUR WORKS;
    MY SOUL KNOWS [YADA] IT VERY WELL.
        (PS. 139:1, 13, 14)

AND THOSE WHO KNOW [YADA] YOUR NAME PUT THEIR
    TRUST IN YOU,
        FOR YOU, O LORD, HAVE NOT FORSAKEN THOSE WHO
        SEEK YOU. (PS. 9:10)

KNOW [YADA] THAT THE LORD, HE IS GOD!
    IT IS HE WHO MADE US, AND WE ARE HIS;
        WE ARE HIS PEOPLE, AND THE SHEEP OF HIS PASTURE.
        (PS. 100:3)

God's heart toward us is so clear in these passages. He doesn't just know about us in a general sense. He knows us deeply and intimately. He formed our inward parts and knitted us together in our mother's womb. He knows us from a Creator's standpoint and from a relational standpoint. We're

His people and the sheep of His pasture. He cares for us deeply. He yadas our very hearts—the souls and cores of our beings. He wants our souls to yada Him—that He is a wonderful God who created us as His wonderful creation. He desires to have a deeper connection with us.

When you rewind the clock and look back at the very first humans ever created, you see that God's intention was to yada humanity all along. Adam and Eve were created to walk and talk with God Himself. No barriers. No issues. Just perfect peace with their Father. God wants the very same thing with us today. He wants a relationship. He wants intimacy. He wants closeness. He wants yada. Ultimately, He sent Jesus to make a way for us to experience that with Him. In an article titled "How to Have Intimacy with God," Jon Bloom of Desiring God writes, "God wants intimacy with you. Christ has done all the hard work in the cross to make it possible. All he requires is that you believe in him (John 14:1). He wants you to trust him with all your heart (Proverbs 3:5). . . . What you must trust God most for right now is where he means for you to draw closer to him."[2]

It's important for us, as women, to understand that we were made for deep intimacy with God. He wants us to trust Him (see Prov. 3:5–6). He wants us to seek Him with all our hearts (see Ps. 27:4). He wants us to thirst for Him as if we were desperate for water (see Ps. 63:1). He wants us to know [yada] that in His presence is fullness of joy (see Ps. 16:11).

If we don't understand how we're meant to relate to God first and foremost, all our relationships, sexual and non-sexual, will struggle. We will never have true intimacy (as God intended) with others unless we understand how to have true intimacy with and to yada God.

Sex and Yada

The day had been a beautiful blur. My white wedding dress blew in the wind as I (Kristen) ran to the getaway car. With my brand-new husband sitting behind the wheel, we roared out of sight. For the first time all day, we were alone. As we drove to our downtown suite, we held hands in excited anticipation of the evening ahead. Neither of us had ever had sex before, so this would be a new chapter in both our lives. After pulling into the parking garage, we grabbed our bags and headed inside. As we got on the elevator, my heart started beating faster. I wasn't nervous . . . *or was I?* I couldn't tell. After entering our honeymoon suite, we just stared at each other. Then Zack wrapped his strong arms around me in a big hug and whispered, "I love you."

The night was filled with romance and passion. It was spectacular.

From that point until now, Zack and I have greatly enjoyed sex within our marriage. It's a wonderful and incredible gift from God. It draws us together. It paves the way for intimacy and love. It unites us in the deepest possible way. Sex is the most personal and vulnerable act either of us has ever experienced with another human. And that's exactly what God intended it to be.

Sex was made for a relationship.

God created sex to thrive in an environment of true love, transparency, commitment, trust, and lifelong covenant love. Sex was made for a relationship. That's why God designed the marriage covenant, then placed sex within it. He created sex to draw a husband and wife together relationally in the deepest possible way.

Sex was created for a wife to *yada* her husband and a husband to *yada* his wife.

God used the word *yada* to describe not only His deep love for us but also something very unexpected. To help us understand the right context and purpose for sex, God intentionally used it to describe *sexual intimacy.* This is truly mind-blowing. Yada changes everything. The deep knowing that God has for His children is the same type of deep knowing that God intends for married couples to have with each other. Sex is supposed to be an expression of the deep knowing and love that a husband and a wife share. As Greg Smalley puts it, "God's idea of yada in marriage is for you to know your spouse completely, for you to be deeply known by your spouse and for both of you to enjoy each other sexually."[3]

Here are a few verses in which yada is used in the context of sexual intimacy:

NOW ADAM KNEW [YADA] EVE HIS WIFE, AND SHE CONCEIVED AND BORE CAIN, SAYING, "I HAVE GOTTEN A MAN WITH THE HELP OF THE LORD." (GEN. 4:1)

CAIN KNEW [YADA] HIS WIFE, AND SHE CONCEIVED AND BORE ENOCH. (GEN. 4:17)

AND THE DAMSEL WAS VERY FAIR TO LOOK UPON, A VIRGIN, NEITHER HAD ANY MAN KNOWN [YADA] HER: AND SHE WENT DOWN TO THE WELL, AND FILLED HER PITCHER, AND CAME UP. (GEN. 24:16 KJV)

Understanding sex within the context of yada changes everything. It unlocks the truth about how God designed sex to be pursued and enjoyed. Because God used the same Hebrew word for God's love and sexual intimacy, we're able to learn big things about both. God's faithful and deep love teaches us about sex, while passionate sex within marriage teaches us about God. Both point to the fact that God is deeply relational and He designed us to be the same. We were made for yada. We were created to be deeply known and loved by our Creator. We were created as sexual beings to be deeply known within a covenant marriage.

Sex is a magnificent gift from God. If we can learn to view it through the lens of yada, it will inform us of so much. We will learn how to cherish it rightly and embrace it within the best context. We will build our marriages on a foundation of transparency, vulnerability, and true, intimate love.

Can't Live without It

We can live without sex, but we can't live without true intimacy. We were made for yada. We were made for deep intimacy with Jesus. When our hearts are filled with a soul-satisfying relationship with Jesus, we have everything we need to thrive. When yada with Jesus becomes a core part of our existence, we view our sexuality through a different lens. We begin to realize that our sexuality enables us to better understand the depth of Christ's love. We can see that sex within marriage is about so much more than going through the motions. It's about deeply knowing the person we're sexually intimate with.

Instead of looking to a mere human to satisfy the deepest longings of your heart, choose to build an intimate relationship with your Savior. Choose to seek Him with all your heart. You were made for intimacy. You were made for yada.

Yada for Single Women (FROM BETHANY)

As I type these words, I'm unmarried, I've never had sex, and I have no real experience in this area. So, what does yada have to do with unmarried women? How can we benefit from this conversation on intimacy? When I first learned about yada, it totally blew me away. I love that God uses the same word to describe both His relationship with us and sexual intimacy. That means single women do not have to wait until marriage to experience yada. We can experience deeply knowing God right now. He created us to be deeply known and to deeply know Him. He wants an intimate relationship with us. When we take a step back and look at the bigger picture, we quickly realize that sex is simply the metaphor that points us toward our deeper need for intimacy with Jesus. The most satisfying thing we can pursue is not a mind-blowing sexual experience but an authentic relationship with our Savior. The next time you feel a sexual urge or wonder if you'll ever experience sexual intimacy, allow those moments to remind you that your truest need is for a relationship with Jesus. Channel the energy you might spend focusing on sexual longings toward knowing Christ deeply and finding ultimate satisfaction in Him.

Yada for married Women (FROM KRISTEN)

As I mentioned before, I experienced sex for the first time on my wedding night with my brand-new husband, Zack. We were young and passionately in love. We enjoyed God's good gift of sexual intimacy with wonder and excitement. However, as the months and years stretched on, I began to notice a distinct pattern. Our sexual relationship was only as good as our emotional relationship. If Zack and I felt relationally disconnected from each another, our sex life wasn't very good. This is when I realized the importance of yada within marriage.

God's purpose for yada in marriage is to draw couples into physical and emotional intimacy. It's a package deal. According to Greg Smalley, "The best sex happens in marriage when a spouse reveals his or her inner world and in response feels fully embraced by his or her mate. This level of vulnerability and acceptance can help you to experience the deepest and most profound intimacy as husband and wife."[4] This is absolutely true for my marriage. When Zack and I pursue a deep connection with each other emotionally and relationally, it always leads to a deeper relationship sexually. The more vulnerable, transparent, and loving we are with each other, the more excited we are to embrace each other sexually.

Marriage thrives when yada is at the core. When a husband and wife know each other deeply, sex becomes the natural and beautiful expression of the intimacy they already share.

8. IMPERFECT PURITY

It was a perfect September evening. I (Kristen) had just finished playing sand volleyball with a group of friends and was headed to grab dinner. As a serious lover of people, sports, and yummy food, this was my ideal way to spend a Friday night. Although dinner was delicious and the friends made great company, someone specific captured my heart that evening. The one and only tall and tanned Zachary Michael Clark was sitting right next to me . . . and boy did I have a serious crush on him. My friends would tease me constantly. I honestly didn't mind the teasing because I was pretty sure Zack liked me back. He hadn't confessed his feelings to me or expressed interest, but I was sure it would happen soon.

After dinner had ended and the last few cars had driven away, the conversation I'd been dying to have with my dream guy actually happened. Little did I know that those few moments of talking with Zack would lead us on a journey toward a relationship that would eventually culminate in marriage.

It's interesting for me to think back on those early days of getting to know Zack. As wonderful as our dating relationship and engagement season were, it wasn't without bumps.

It wasn't without growing pains. It wasn't without long conversations and learning curves. Many of those discussions revolved around purity.

During our dating relationship, Zack and I genuinely desired to honor God. We both wanted to pursue purity in our relationship. However, our motives for embracing purity weren't always right. Instead of pursuing purity out of a heart to honor God, we were often more focused on "following the rules." As our relationship progressed, we realized how wrong our motives truly were. We slowly learned that true purity wasn't about the dos and don'ts. It wasn't about looking good in front of others. It wasn't about taking pride in our abstinence. We realized that we should be motivated to pursue true biblical purity because of our desire to honor God in all areas of our lives—from our actions to our thoughts to our choices. Biblical purity is about so much more than obeying a list of rules.

Biblical purity is about so much more than obeying a list of rules.

WRONG NARRATIVES ABOUT PURITY

You've probably heard the words *purity* or *sexual purity* at some point in your life. Maybe you heard them from your pastor, your parents, your boyfriend, or a book you read. Depending on our individual upbringings, sexual purity can mean something different to each of us. If you grew up in a home where people rarely talked about anything sexual and your parents simply emphasized not to have sex until you're married, you might have a negative view of purity. If you were taught that purity was the most important thing in a woman's life, you may view it as the most noble thing a woman could pursue. If you were taught that "true love waits" but then had sex before marriage, you might feel shame every time you hear the word. Maybe you weren't taught anything about sexual purity, so this is an entirely new concept for you.

Regardless of your upbringing or current perspective on purity, let's take a step back and rethink this term altogether. When we, as imperfect women, embrace a view of purity that doesn't line up with God's Word, it can be very damaging to us.

Let's look at some of the most common yet false narratives surrounding purity today.

Wrong Narrative #1: Sex Is a Bad and Scary Thing

Don't talk about sex, don't think about sex, and don't you dare have sex. Sex is considered a big no-no in this purity narrative. It's a hush-hush topic that you're not supposed to even think about until you get married. But once you're married, you're supposed to have a radical shift in your perspective and unwrap the beautiful gift of sex on your wedding night. It's no wonder this narrative often produces a terrible perspective of sex for many women. Sex goes from something scary and bad to something suddenly beautiful and good. That's a hard switch for any woman to make.

This purity narrative is completely anti-God and has absolutely no biblical framework. Sex should never be cast in a bad or scary light. If this is your perspective of purity, then your choice to abstain from sex will most likely be rooted in fear. You'll be left wondering things such as *If sex is such a bad and scary thing, then why did*

Sex should never be cast in a bad or scary light.

God create me with longings? Why did He give me desires if they are so wrong?

Instead of embracing this wrong narrative, we need to reject it. It's not biblical—or helpful.

Wrong Narrative #2: Your Worth Is Based on Your Level of Pureness

Imagine living a life in which you always strived to earn God's love. When you did good, acted good, and looked good, He loved you. When you did bad, acted bad, and looked bad, He didn't love you. That would be an awful way to experience love. If you, as a woman, have to earn your worth through performance or good actions, then that's not a true depiction of love. That's a conditional relationship. The apostle Paul writes, "But God shows his love for us in that while we were still sinners, Christ died for us" (Rom. 5:8).

Sadly, many of us view sexual purity through a similar lens. We equate our worth in God's eyes to our level of "pureness." Instead of making choices out of a desire to love and glorify God, we make choices out of a works-based mindset. We believe we need to earn our worth and credibility in God's eyes.

What a terrible and anti-gospel message.

God has no ranking systems. He doesn't decide certain categories of people based on who's lived a "pure" life and who hasn't. If we, as women, have the ability to contribute to or take away from our worth, the gospel is meaningless. Jesus's death on the cross would have been pointless. We need to remember that every single one of us is incredibly imperfect and in desperate need of Christ and His perfection. We're all impure before God (see Isa. 64:6). We all need His saving grace and perfect righteousness to make us pure. Instead of striving to earn our worth through our purity, let's accept the worth Christ has already given us. We don't have to earn it; He gives it freely.

Wrong Narrative #3: Purity Is for Single People Only

I can't wait to get married. I won't have to worry about purity anymore. All my sexual desires will be satisfied and I'll no longer struggle with any of my previous lusts or unfulfilled longings. Those are the thoughts of many single women. They believe purity is only something to be embraced prior to marriage.

That's far from the truth.

If we, as women, view purity through a "for only single people" lens, we will assume marriage will solve all our sexual problems. We will assume that having sex will fix us. We will count on marriage to cure our addictions, temptations, and just make life so much easier. This couldn't be further from the truth. Sex won't fix your problems. Marriage won't erase your addictions.

This is why purity isn't for only single women. It's for all women. It's so important to remember that sexual temptation is a reality for everyone during every season of life. It comes in different shapes and sizes, but it's something we will always face. If we don't learn to view purity as something that must be pursued during singleness and after singleness, we will be in for a major surprise. Just think about how many marriages suffer from porn addictions, adultery, lust, and other sexual sins. Married people need God's help to pursue a heart of purity just as much as single people.

Now that we've explored three of the wrong narratives surrounding purity, let's take a look at what God's Word actually teaches.

Sex won't fix your problems.

Biblical Narrative: PURSUING PURITY OUT OF A HEART THAT DESIRES TO HONOR GOD

Imagine a woman who understands that she is imperfect but strives to honor God with her heart, mind, and soul. Her actions in private and in public flow from a heart that's fully reliant on Christ. She counts on Christ to help her fight sexual temptation and she accepts God's forgiveness when she stumbles and falls. She gets that she's imperfect. She gets that she needs God's strength to help her win the battle. She gets that purity is about so much more than earning her worth or looking good in front of other people. She gets that her life is about living for Christ and choosing to become holy as God is holy. This is a woman who understands a biblical definition of purity.

If we, as women, want to embrace purity as God designed it, we must first acknowledge that we're imperfect. In and of ourselves, we're completely impure and unable to change that. This is what Dr. Juli Slattery has to say about sexual purity:

> The fact is that none of us is 100% sexually pure—we have all missed God's "plan A" of perfection. Our purity according to Scripture is determined by the blood of Jesus Christ, not by our sexual choices. There are not some women who need Jesus more than others. As the Bible says, all of us have sinned and are "dirty" before God. It is only Jesus' atoning death on the cross that supernaturally presents us as a pure and spotless Bride.[1]

That must be our starting place. We must acknowledge our need for Jesus. We must accept His perfect righteousness in place of our imperfect lives.

Once you've accepted that you are imperfect and in need of Christ's perfection, your focus will totally change. Instead of striving to live up to some impossible standard of perfection, you will recognize your need for Jesus. Your entire life is about accepting His grace and walking in that new identity. You are no longer just an imperfect woman. You are an imperfect woman with a perfect Savior. He equips you to fight the battle. He offers you forgiveness over and over again. He gives you His identity as a daughter of God (see John 1:12). Your life's aim is about worshiping God above all else. First Peter 1:15–16 says, "But just as he who called you is holy, so be holy in all you do: for it is written: 'Be holy, because I am holy'" (NIV).

Sexual purity is not just about saying no to sex before marriage; it's about taking every thought captive and living in a way that reflects the perfect holiness of your Father. It's ultimately about embracing your identity as a daughter of God and striving every day to become more like Him. That's true purity. That's the identity God has called you to walk in.

You are an imperfect woman with a perfect Savior.

A Daughter of God

Regardless of the narrative you grew up with, we hope you can see that true purity isn't about achieving some status of perfection. The goal of purity is to surrender your heart, life, and sexuality to God on a daily basis in order to live for His kingdom purposes. It's about using your body in a way that's in line with your identity as God's daughter. By God's grace, He has given you the power to embrace a heart of purity and holiness for His glory.

Part three

What Every Girl
Needs to Know

9. BATTLING TEMPTATION

When I (Kristen) was a teenager, it felt as though the entire world was talking about this one particular newly released movie. I loved watching movies as much as the next girl and was dying to join the fun. Plus, this one featured some of the hottest Hollywood actors, so I was sure it would be good. After seeing the trailer online, my excitement was suddenly met with feelings of annoyance. I knew my parents wouldn't want me to watch the film because of its heavy seductive and sensual themes. Deep in my heart, I knew watching it probably wasn't a "good" choice . . . but I still wanted to see it.

A few weeks went by and I continued to read and hear more about this movie. By this point, I felt as if I was the only person on earth who hadn't seen it.

Instead of moving on and just forgetting about the movie altogether, I continued to think about it daily. *If only I could watch it. Ugh, why are my parents so old-fashioned?* And then an idea hit me. I had a master plan. Maybe my parents didn't need to know about this movie. Maybe I didn't need to tell them anything about it. With that thought taking root in my brain, I smiled. Once the movie released into stores, I would buy it and secretly watch it in my room (this was before online streaming existed, of course). No one would ever know. My plan was perfect.

The moment the movie hit store shelves, I was there. I bought it and tucked it deep inside my big leather purse. Late that night, when everyone was asleep, I watched the movie. My long-anticipated moment had come.

I woke up the next morning feeling a mixture of emotions. Although I had gotten my way, I didn't feel satisfied. I felt guilty. I knew the stuff I'd seen on that little screen in the privacy of my room wasn't good. It wasn't pure. It wasn't God-honoring. Instead of feeling excited and thrilled with my choice, I felt ashamed. I felt convicted about what I'd done.

As the day slowly dragged on, a thought washed over me. *I should be honest about what I had done.* I had gone behind my parents' backs and watched something they wouldn't have liked. Not only had I deceived them, but I had also sinned against God in the process.

Although giving into the temptation felt sweet in the moment, it wasn't worth it in the long run.

What Is Temptation?

Temptation is something every single one of us faces on a regular basis. It's part of living in a fallen world, having an enemy, and being born a sinner. Since temptation is so prevalent in our lives, it's crucial that we have a biblical understanding of exactly what it is and how it works. According to Pastor Steven J. Cole, "By understanding how temptation works we can devise a strategy for victory over it. To be forewarned of Satan's strategy is to be forearmed. His pattern for tempting Eve is essentially the same approach he uses today. By studying and learning to recognize that pattern, we will not be ignorant of his schemes (2 Cor. 2:11), and thus can resist them."[1]

That's the goal of trying to understand temptation—to be forewarned so we can be forearmed. When we take the time to slow down and learn how temptation works, we will become better prepared for the battle. The two of us love the way Puritan theologian John Owen describes temptation. Although he penned these words over three hundred years ago, they are still relevant for us today: "A temptation, then, in general is anything that, for any reason, exerts a force or influence to seduce and draw the mind and heart of man from the obedience which God requires of him to any kind of sin."[2] This is exactly what temptation looks like for us today. Temptation draws our hearts and minds away from glorifying God and toward satisfying our own sinful desires. It encourages us to question God's authority and consider the possibility of a better way. Temptation promises that if we just "take a bite," we'll find what we're truly looking for.

To be forewarned of Satan's strategy is to be forearmed.
—Steven J. Cole

Before we dig into how temptation works, let's first look at six biblical facts about temptation to better understand it.

SIX BIBLICAL FACTS ABOUT TEMPTATION

1. WE ALL FACE TEMPTATION ON THIS EARTH. NO ONE IS IMMUNE TO IT (SEE 1 COR. 10:13).
2. CHRIST CAN SYMPATHIZE WITH US BECAUSE HE WAS TEMPTED WHILE HE LIVED ON THE EARTH (SEE HEB. 4:15).

3. TEMPTATION DOES NOT EQUAL SIN. CHRIST WAS TEMPTED, BUT HE NEVER SINNED (SEE HEB. 4:15).

4. GOD DOES NOT TEMPT US, BUT HE DOES ALLOW US TO BE TEMPTED BY THE ENEMY AND BY OUR OWN SINFUL HEARTS (SEE JAMES 1:13-14).

5. WE HAVE A REAL ENEMY SEEKING TO STEAL, KILL, AND DESTROY US. HIS GOAL IS TO DRAW US INTO SIN AND AWAY FROM GOD (SEE 1 PET. 5:8).

6. IT'S POSSIBLE TO RESIST TEMPTATION. CHRIST LIVED ON THE EARTH, WAS TEMPTED, AND NEVER SINNED. AS CHRISTIANS, WE HAVE THE ABILITY THROUGH CHRIST'S POWER TO DO AS HE DID. WE HAVE THE VICTORY THROUGH CHRIST (SEE MATT. 4:1-11).

How Temptation Works

When it comes to how temptation works, the Bible unpacks it simply and clearly. According to James 1:13–15, "Let no one say when he is tempted, 'I am being tempted by God,' for God cannot be tempted with evil, and he himself tempts no one. But each person is tempted when he is lured and enticed by his own desire. Then desire when it has conceived gives birth to sin, and sin when it is fully grown brings forth death."

Sadly, the story of Eve is one of the clearest examples of what this verse looks like when lived out in real life. She did exactly what it says not to do. She willingly lingered in the presence of temptation, listened to the lies of the enemy, pondered the serpent's deceitful words, and then chose to accept the fruit.

Eve is not alone in her actions though. Every single day, millions of women (the two of us included) do exactly what Eve did. We listen, we ponder, we take, and we believe the enemy's lies and give into temptation. We grab that juicy piece of fruit (porn, masturbation, erotica, adultery, sex before marriage, etc.), we bite into its offers of pleasure, we swallow, and then we feel the pain and brokenness of that sin. The flavor turns sour in our mouth and we wish we could spit it back out. But we can't.

Think about what happens when you're tempted to sin sexually. Maybe you're hit with a strong temptation to look at porn. It sounds so satisfying in the moment, but you know it always leaves you wanting more. Maybe you're lying in bed when all of a sudden you're overwhelmed with a desire to masturbate. It feels so relieving in the moment, but the satisfaction of the action never lasts. Maybe you see a hot surfer dude at the beach and you're tempted to fantasize about him. You enjoy lusting after his body but feel empty when the moment of pleasure passes. Whatever the temptation may be, each one starts with an initial thought or desire. You want, you look, and you ponder. Temptation offers you a juicy piece of fruit with alluring promises of satisfaction but leaves you empty and broken inside.

We listen, we ponder, we take, and we believe the enemy's lies and give into temptation.

Instead of continuing to face temptation empty-handed, we need to grab some ammo. We need to understand how temptation works so we can fight the battle in a more biblical and effective way. We are going to use James 1, as well as the story of Eve, to unpack the three-step process of temptation. This will show you clearly how temptation works and equip you to spot temptation the moment it presents itself in your life.

THREE-STEP PROCESS OF TEMPTATION

Step 1: Listen

Think about what happened to Eve on the day she ate the forbidden fruit (see Gen. 3:6). She knew exactly where that tree was in the Garden. Instead of avoiding it, she walked toward it. She lingered in its presence and listened to the serpent's voice (see v. 5). She allowed Satan to fan the flame of her desire for the forbidden. The longer she listened, the greater her desire grew.

In that moment of initial temptation, Eve could have run. She could have fled from Satan's presence. But she didn't. Instead, she lingered and allowed Satan to lure her into his wicked schemes. She listened to her desires and allowed them to overtake what she knew was right because God had told her so. In a sense, she followed her heart.

The first step of temptation is listening to your desires. A desire for more. A desire for something different. A desire for satisfaction. A desire for pleasure. When the desire presents itself (whether internally in our thoughts or externally by someone or something), we have a choice. We can listen to the desire and pour fuel on the fire or we can squelch it and run. James notes that "each person is tempted when he is lured and enticed by his own desire" (1:14). Eve allowed herself to be lured and tempted. This was her very first mistake. As Nancy Wolgemuth says so well, "Eve's first mistake was not eating the fruit; her first mistake was listening to the serpent."[3]

Think about it this way. You meet a really cute guy at a coffee shop and realize you have a lot of similar interests. A few weeks go by and you exchange numbers. A few more weeks go by and you begin texting each other on a regular basis. One evening, he texts you a complimentary message and asks you for some photos. You know what he wants. He wants you to send him some nudes. You stare at the message and reread his seemingly sweet words over and over again. You think about the fact that he wants to see you. The more you listen to your thoughts, the more you consider sending him the photos.

When we listen to temptation, we take our first wrong step. Once we allow a desire to linger in our minds, we begin to ponder what we're hearing. Instead of nipping temptation in the bud, we allow it to take us straight to step two in the three-step process of temptation.

Step 2: Ponder

When you stop and think about the word *ponder*, you'll realize it's exactly what Eve did in the Garden. After she saw the serpent in the tree, she engaged in a conversation with him. "He [Satan] said to the woman, 'Did God actually say, "You shall not eat of any tree in the garden"?' And the woman *said* to the serpent . . ." (Gen. 3:1–2, italics added). Did you catch that? Eve responded. She listened to what he was saying and *pondered* his words. She didn't run away from him. She talked with him. She allowed herself to be enticed by his offer.

Temptation always works this way. It starts slow. It gets us to think. To question. To reconsider what God might have said. Temptation presents itself as offering something we must have to be happy. It appeals to our inner flesh. The more we allow ourselves to ponder the temptation and think about how wonderful it might be, the further we step into it.

Imagine it this way. You're in your bedroom late at night and the desire to look at porn hits you strong. You allow the thought to linger in your mind and then you grab your cell phone. You stare at the black screen and begin to imagine how satisfying it would feel to have just a peek. Deep in your heart, you know porn is wrong and sinful, but the desire to look is so intense. Instead of dropping your phone and resisting the temptation, you allow yourself to look at your phone and scroll through the apps. You ponder the desire more and more. Before you know it, several minutes have gone by and you are now deep in the throes of sin.

Pondering temptation almost always leads straight into step three of the three-step process of temptation.

Step 3: Accept

The fruit looked delicious. Eve stood there long enough to smell its fragrance. She desired to taste it. She listened to the serpent long enough to be deceived by his sly words.

One little step at a time and Eve eventually accepted Satan's word over God's. After lingering in the fruit's presence, she took a bite. She ate. After she tasted the fruit for herself, she handed it to her husband and he ate as well (see Gen. 3:6). The deed had been done. The temptation had been acted on. The lie had been believed. One step at a time, sin had been conceived. "Desire when it has conceived gives birth to sin" (James 1:15).

Accepting the offer is the final step in the three-step process of temptation.

What starts out as a thought, a glance, a desire, ultimately turns into an acceptance of that temptation. In his article "The 4 Stages of Temptation," Dan Armstrong says it this way:

> Now, after putting feet to your desires, you get closer and closer to the moment of indulgence, and then you do. You indulge. The space between conception and birth might take a day, hours, or maybe only minutes, but birth is the natural

follow-through of conception. This is the next stage of what James calls the birth of sin. We give into the temptation fully and we start looking at porn or we start engaging in sinful sexual behavior of some kind.[4]

Most of us do not go from simply desiring to actually accepting the fruit in one single moment. It's typically a process. Just like Eve, we take one small step at a time. We listen with our ears, ponder in our hearts, and make a choice that ultimately leads to sin.

Result: Sin

Giving into temptation always results in sin. We reject God's Word in some sort of way. In Eve's world, sin was unheard of. No one had ever sinned against God. When sin entered the world for the very first time, death entered the picture as well. "Sin when it is fully grown brings forth death" (James 1:15). No longer would Adam and Eve live in perfect bodies. They would eventually die, and the entire world now follows in their footsteps.

Dan Armstrong writes, "Now, we know the wages of sin is death in an ultimate sense—this is the consequence of sin God warned us about long ago before our first parents sinned in Eden. But in the Bible, death isn't merely the final stop of life. It's a word used to describe the whole process of decay and misery that results from sin."[5]

Think about what happens after you indulge in lust. Does that action bring you life? Does it satisfy you long term? Does it quench your ultimate desire for peace and joy? It might for a fleeting moment, but it doesn't ultimately satisfy. It can't. Instead, it does the opposite. It leaves you worse off than you were before. It leaves you feeling broken, depressed, alone, guilty, ashamed, and wishing you had never given in.

It's crucial to remember that temptation never shows us the end result—sin and consequences—when it first presents itself. If it did, we'd never give in. We'd avoid it and run away. Instead, temptation is always wrapped in an enticing covering of lies. It's sneaky, deceptive, and filled with promises it can't keep. When we understand the result of giving into temptation, it should give us a whole lot more pause. It should cause us to consider the end result.

Instead of focusing on the momentary pleasures temptation offers us, we must be vigilant to think through all three steps in the process. Let's remember what happens as a result of giving into temptation. If we're willing to consider the full process and honestly acknowledge the result of sin, temptation will become easier to spot and avoid.

She Wanted and He Resisted

We've talked a lot about Eve and the results of her actions. She wanted the fruit and the freedom she thought it would offer her. She walked through every single step of the temptation process and ended up dying—both spiritually and physically. Her life and world were total wrecks after she gave into temptation.

There's another person in the Bible who was also greatly tempted. However, this person did the exact opposite of what Eve did. Instead of pondering in the presence of desire, this man fled from it. If you've ever heard the story of Joseph in the Old Testament, you probably know exactly what we're talking about. He was faced with one serious temptation but did not give into it (you can read the full story in Genesis 39).

After a series of events, Joseph became a slave in Egypt. He was a well-off slave because he was working for Potiphar, the captain of the palace guard. One afternoon, Potiphar's wife (a woman of great power and influence) presented Joseph with a tempting offer. This woman thought Joseph was one hunk of a man and wanted to have sex with him. Potiphar's wife had worked out a strategic plan by sending all the servants out for the afternoon to make sure the house was empty. When Joseph came into the house to do his work, only Potiphar's wife was there. She grabbed Joseph by his shirt and begged him to sleep with her. She was desperate to satisfy her sexual lust with Joseph. Instead of giving in and obeying his master's wife, Joseph chose to honor the Lord. He said, "No one is greater in this house than I am. My master has withheld nothing from me except you, because you are his wife. How then could I do such a wicked thing and sin against God?" (Gen. 39:9 NIV). Joseph then fled from the scene and ran from the face of temptation. He didn't allow his sinful desires to kick in. He didn't stand there and allow her to woo him. He didn't ponder the momentary pleasures of lust.

No. He did the opposite. He literally ran from temptation. Joseph ran from that woman and didn't look back.

Years later, God used Joseph to save the Israelites from a famine. Joseph's faithfulness to God resulted in literally thousands of people being saved from starvation. What a different outcome from the results of Eve's choice. One decision brought death and the other brought life. Eve and Joseph faced the same choice—to give into temptation and the flesh or to resist it and honor God.

Joseph ran from that woman and didn't look back.

Run from Temptation

Think about your own life. When was the last time you gave into sexual temptation? When the temptation first presented itself, what did you do? What did that process look like? Were you by yourself? Were you with a group of friends? Were you doing something you knew could potentially cause temptation? As you look back on that specific situation, think about what you could have done differently. How could you have resisted?

The more you understand the process of how you gave into that temptation, the easier it will be to spot temptation in the future.

Here are a few ways you can run from temptation the next time it happens.

IF YOU'RE TEMPTED TO SEND A GUY NUDE PHOTOS, DELETE HIS MESSAGE AND CALL A GODLY WOMAN FOR HELP. DON'T LINGER ON HIS MESSAGE. RUN FROM IT.

IF YOU'RE TEMPTED TO LOOK AT PORN ONLINE, CHOOSE TO IM-MEDIATELY SHUT OFF YOUR DEVICE. DON'T ALLOW YOURSELF TO BROWSE THE WEB. RUN FROM IT.

IF YOUR BOYFRIEND IS CONSTANTLY TEMPTING YOU TO HAVE SEX WITH HIM, END THE RELATIONSHIP. DON'T WELCOME THAT KIND OF PRESSURE INTO YOUR LIFE. RUN FROM IT.

IF YOU'RE TEMPTED TO READ EROTICA, GET RID OF EVERY BIT OF EROTICA YOU OWN BY THROWING IT AWAY OR DELETING IT. DON'T KEEP THAT CONTENT AROUND. RUN FROM IT.

In all this, remember that being forewarned is being fore-armed. Our hope for you is that by reading this chapter, you will be forearmed and equipped to run from sexual temp-tation. Don't do what Eve did. Do the opposite. Run. Run from that lustful desire. Run from its enticing offer and don't look back.

10. THE SECRET STRUGGLE WITHIN YOUR MIND

Fantasizing was my (Bethany's) specialty. I would lie in bed at night and fantasize about guys for hours on end. I would fantasize about kissing. I would fantasize about sex. I would imagine the perfect fairy-tale romance and I would be the star of the show.

It wasn't until I hit my later teen years that I finally began to see the hypocrisy of my fantasies. I was living a pure life outwardly, but inwardly I was struggling. My outward actions were not a true reflection of my heart. I needed to begin embracing purity from the inside out.

Thankfully, God knew just what I needed during that season of my life. I ended up reading a Christian book that addressed exactly what I was dealing with. The author talked about the need to have a pure heart as well as pure actions. My thoughts needed to be filled with love for Jesus, not dominated by sexual fantasies.

The book ended with several points of practical application. This was gold for me. I needed the truth, but I also needed the practical. Slowly but surely I began to make choices that impacted me from the inside out. My heart was being transformed and I saw the need to live a pure life in my mind as well as in my actions.

Fine Outwardly, Struggling Inwardly

While writing this book, the two of us quickly realized we aren't the only ones who've struggled with inner purity. We aren't the only ones who've looked good on the outside but battled to remain pure on the inside. Here's what a few of you had to say about your internal struggle:

"Keeping my thoughts pure is the most challenging thing about pursuing purity." —Hailey

"I've never experienced much temptation for physical purity. But the battle for purity in my mind and heart is constant. In the past, I've struggled a lot to keep my thoughts pure and honorable toward God and the men in my life in the midst of a sex-saturated world." —Jasmin

"I think with a guy, I can easily say no to the physical. However, in my mind the guy and I have already gone way further than I would have ever considered going before marriage." —Morgan

"It's so easy to let my mind wander. I start building scenes and slowly allow things to unfold. I need to learn how to take every thought captive to the obedience of Christ." —Janice

The battle for inner purity is something many of us face on a daily basis. We find it easy to say no to the physical but struggle to keep our inner thoughts honoring toward Christ. We might look put together on the outside, but it's not an accurate reflection of what's on the inside.

I (Kristen) recently talked with a young woman who was dealing with this exact issue. Everyone around her thought she was incredibly godly and held her up as an example of purity. Her parents bragged about her to their parent friends. But every time her parents spoke to others about how godly and pure she was, she wanted to run and cry. She knew her heart wasn't pure. She looked like a good church girl on the outside but was giving into lust on the inside. Only she knew the reality of her struggles.

The battle for inner purity is something many of us face on a daily basis.

As Christian women, we may find it hard to admit our internal struggles when everyone around us thinks we're doing amazing. It can be hard to open up and ask for help when the people around us admire our "godliness."

I (Bethany) remember feeling this same struggle. As a Christian girl who looked as though she had it altogether on the outside, I was too ashamed to be transparent about what was really going on. As much as I wanted to keep my sin a secret, I knew I wasn't being honest. I also knew God saw the depths of my heart and nothing was hidden from Him.

God Knows It All

Sometimes it can be easy to pretend we're doing better than we actually are. We easily deceive ourselves and others into thinking we've got things figured out. Other people can't see inside of us, so they don't know if we're truly doing well or if we're struggling. However, keeping our inner struggles a secret isn't helpful to us and it isn't helpful to those trying to help us. And the reality is, God already knows everything about us (see Ps. 38:9). He understands the condition of our hearts. He sees our struggles. He's aware of every thought that enters our brains. He's not surprised by our good or bad deeds.

> You know when I sit down and when I rise up;
>   you discern my thoughts from afar.
> You search out my path and my lying down
>   and are acquainted with all my ways.
> Even before a word is on my tongue,
>   behold, O Lord, you know it altogether.
> (Ps. 139:2–4)

When it comes to the battle for our inner purity, we may find it difficult to gauge how much we're actually struggling. Outward actions are easy to measure. Thoughts, desires, emotions, and longings are a whole lot more difficult to quantify. That's one of the reasons it's so easy to keep our inward struggles a secret.

God already knows everything about us.

Using the measuring chart on the next page, mark the line according to how much you're wrestling with each issue.

The Secret Struggle Heart Check

1. IMAGINING AND DREAMING ABOUT SEX IN MY MIND

   1 . . . . . 2 . . . . . 3 . . . . . 4 . . . . . 5 . . . . . 6 . . . . . 7 . . . . . 8 . . . . . 9 10
   Not struggling   Majorly struggling

2. CREATING SEXUAL FANTASY STORIES

   1 . . . . . 2 . . . . . 3 . . . . . 4 . . . . . 5 . . . . . 6 . . . . . 7 . . . . . 8 . . . . . 9 10
   Not struggling   Majorly struggling

3. DAYDREAMING ABOUT BEING MARRIED AND HAVING SEX WITH MY FUTURE HUSBAND

   1 . . . . . 2 . . . . . 3 . . . . . 4 . . . . . 5 . . . . . 6 . . . . . 7 . . . . . 8 . . . . . 9 10
   Not struggling   Majorly struggling

4. DAYDREAMING ABOUT HAVING SEX WITH SOMEONE ELSE'S HUSBAND

   1 . . . . . 2 . . . . . 3 . . . . . 4 . . . . . 5 . . . . . 6 . . . . . 7 . . . . . 8 . . . . . 9 10
   Not struggling   Majorly struggling

5. RELIVING SEXUAL EXPERIENCES IN MY MIND THAT I'VE SEEN OTHERS ACT OUT

   1 . . . . . 2 . . . . . 3 . . . . . 4 . . . . . 5 . . . . . 6 . . . . . 7 . . . . . 8 . . . . . 9 10
   Not struggling   Majorly struggling

6. MAKING OUT WITH MY CRUSH OR BOYFRIEND IN MY MIND

   1 . . . . . 2 . . . . . 3 . . . . . 4 . . . . . 5 . . . . . 6 . . . . . 7 . . . . . 8 . . . . . 9 10
   Not struggling   Majorly struggling

7. WRITING SEXUALLY EXPLICIT STORIES

   1 . . . . . 2 . . . . . 3 . . . . . 4 . . . . . 5 . . . . . 6 . . . . . 7 . . . . . 8 . . . . . 9 10
   Not struggling   Majorly struggling

8. WATCHING SHOWS OR MOVIES THAT FUEL MY SEXUAL PASSIONS

   1 . . . . . 2 . . . . . 3 . . . . . 4 . . . . . 5 . . . . . 6 . . . . . 7 . . . . . 8 . . . . . 9 10
   Not struggling   Majorly struggling

9. LISTENING TO SEXUALLY CHARGED MUSIC

   1 . . . . . 2 . . . . . 3 . . . . . 4 . . . . . 5 . . . . . 6 . . . . . 7 . . . . . 8 . . . . . 9 10
   Not struggling   Majorly struggling

10. PRETENDING TO LIVE A PURE LIFE ON THE OUTSIDE WHILE STRUGGLING WITH PURITY ON THE INSIDE

   1 . . . . . 2 . . . . . 3 . . . . . 4 . . . . . 5 . . . . . 6 . . . . . 7 . . . . . 8 . . . . . 9 10
   Not struggling   Majorly struggling

Once you've marked each one of your answers, take this list before God in prayer. Remember that He already knows your struggles. They don't surprise Him. Confess your inner struggles to Him and ask for forgiveness. Ask Him to help you pursue purity in these secret areas of your heart. Ask Him to strengthen you from the inside out. We'll dig deeper into how to apply this practically in your life at the end of this chapter.

UNDERSTANDING THE DEPTHS OF YOUR HEART

If we want genuine freedom from our secret struggles, we need to understand a biblical view of the heart. We need to understand who God created us to be on the inside. To fight our secret sins more effectively, we need to better understand where the struggle is taking place inside of us. Is the struggle happening in our thoughts? What about our hearts? How do emotions play into it? Do I just need to stop doing certain things? How can I love God with all my heart when my heart is struggling? What about my will? Do I have a choice in all of this? Biblical counselor Elyse Fitzpatrick says that when the Bible refers to the heart, it's referencing the three main parts of our inner selves: the mind, the affections, and the will. She breaks it down this way:

The mind

The term *heart* refers first to our minds, which includes our thoughts, beliefs, understandings, memories, judgments, conscience, and discernment (see 1 Kings 3:12; Matt. 13:15; Luke 24:38; Rom. 1:21; 1 Tim. 1:5).

The Affections

Another part of our inner person or heart is our affections. Our affections include our desires, feelings, imaginations, and emotions (see Deut. 28:47; Josh. 14:8; 1 Sam. 1:8; Pss. 20:4; 73:7; James 3:14).

The Will

The third way our hearts function is the will. The will is the part of our inner person that chooses or determines what actions we take. The will is informed by the mind and the affections about the best course of action, and then the will acts upon it (Deut. 30:19; Josh. 24:15; Ps. 25:12; Isa. 7:15).[1]

When we think about our own inner struggles, we can think of them happening within the context of our minds, affections, and will. Fitzpatrick describes it this way: "Your mind should inform your affections of the source of your highest happiness; your affections imagine it, cause you to long for it, and apply the impetus needed to awaken your will to choose."[2]

If our minds dwell on lustful thoughts, it will only fuel lustful affections. The more we think about those lustful thoughts, the more we will long for them. The more we long for them, the easier it will be to replay them over and over in our minds. To change this pattern and begin living pure from the inside out, we must fuel our minds with Christ-centered truths. The more we fill our minds with pure thoughts, the more our affections will desire godly things. The more our

If our minds dwell on lustful thoughts, it will only fuel lustful affections.

affections long for Christ and His righteousness, the more we will choose Him over our fantasies.

Since your heart encompasses your mind, your affections, and your will, it's important to view your inner self with all three aspects in mind. As you strive to make a change in the secret areas of your life, it is so important to understand the full spectrum of who you are on the inside so you can better pursue real and lasting change.

Remember, in all this, your goal isn't just to achieve a status of purity but to align your entire life, inner and outer, with the great and first commandment in the Bible: "You shall love the Lord your God with all your heart and with all your soul and with all your mind. This is the great and first commandment" (Matt. 22:37–38). To love the Lord your God with all your heart, soul, and mind is the goal in achieving inner purity.

STRATEGIES TO WIN THE INNER STRUGGLE

When I (Bethany) began to realize my inner struggle for purity, I knew that I needed a specific battle plan to help me gain victory. I'm going to share with you five very specific and practical strategies I put into action to help me with my inner struggles. These strategies guided me toward loving Christ with all my heart, soul, and mind.

Purge

Purging your life of anything that isn't helping you in your battle for inner purity is crucial (see Ps. 32:5). Remember that your mind is one of the key aspects of your heart. If you're fueling your mind with immoral and impure content, you're going to continue to struggle. Get serious about getting serious. Put your desire for purity into action by purging unhelpful content from your life.

To purge items from my life, I did a few things. I took a big black trash bag and went into my bedroom. I seriously evaluated everything in there. I looked through my books, movies, music, magazines, clothes, etc., and put everything that was a hindrance to me in the trash bag. Even if it was just a small hindrance, I got rid of it. Then I took that bag, drove it down the street, and threw it away. I didn't want any of those things in my room anymore.

Remember that your mind is one of the key aspects of your heart.

Next, I went on my cell phone and computer. I scrolled through all my apps, social media outlets, and subscriptions and purged anything that wasn't helpful for me. I unfollowed people, unsubscribed from emails, and deleted music, shows, and anything that wasn't aiding me in my fight for purity.

If you're serious about fighting for inner purity, get serious about purging. Don't leave anything that's even a slight temptation. Get rid of everything and don't look back.

Study

Studying God's Word for yourself is essential in your fight for inner purity. The Bible is unlike any other book on earth. It's God's inspired Word given to us so we would know what is right and true. According to the Bible, "All Scripture is breathed out by God and profitable for teaching, for reproof, for correction, and for training in righteousness, that the man of God may be complete, equipped for every good work" (2 Tim. 3:16–17).

Reading the Bible can often feel like an overwhelming task. It's a huge book and has a lot of different parts to it. It's divided into the Old and New Testament and is filled with history, poetry, prophecy, wisdom, and so much more. So, where should you start?

Thankfully, there isn't one perfect method for reading the Bible. There are many wonderful and helpful ways to go about studying it. If you have a current Bible reading program that works well for you, stick with that. If you need a suggestion, I recommend starting with the book of Proverbs. It's a small book, only thirty-one chapters, filled with practical wisdom. Since a calendar month typically has thirty-one days, it's easy to read one Proverb a day.

Pull out your Bible (or use a free one online) and open up to the book of Proverbs. Read the proverb that coincides with the calendar day for today. If it's the fifteenth, read Proverbs 15. If it's the twenty-ninth, read Proverbs 29. It's that simple. Do this every day for the next thirty-one days as a great way to begin studying the Bible.

Memorize

Getting into God's Word and memorizing different passages from Scripture is one of the best ways to renew your mind (see Rom. 12:2). It's so satisfying to get your mind off life's distractions and instead focus completely on God. When you memorize something, it becomes easily accessible anytime and anyplace. Memorizing Scripture means you can take it with you anywhere you go.

Thanks to my parents, I grew up memorizing many Bible verses. Having personal experience in this area, I can say memorizing Scripture is absolutely worth the effort. If you don't already memorize on a regular basis, I encourage you to begin doing it. Here are a few great passages to help you get started.

> Create in me a clean heart, O God,
>   and renew a right spirit within me. (Ps. 51:10)

No temptation has overtaken you that is not common to man. God is faithful, and he will not let you be tempted beyond your ability, but with the temptation he will also provide the way of escape, that you may be able to endure it. (1 Cor. 10:13)

Bethany's FAVORITE BIBLE VERSE:

TRUST IN THE LORD WITH ALL YOUR HEART,
    AND DO NOT LEAN ON YOUR OWN UNDERSTANDING.
IN ALL YOUR WAYS ACKNOWLEDGE HIM,
    AND HE WILL MAKE STRAIGHT YOUR PATHS.
(PROV. 3:5-6)

Kristen's FAVORITE BIBLE VERSE:

WORTHY ARE YOU, OUR LORD AND GOD,
    TO RECEIVE GLORY AND HONOR AND POWER,
FOR YOU CREATED ALL THINGS,
    AND BY YOUR WILL THEY EXISTED AND WERE CREATED.
(REV. 4:11)

Strategize

Consider your life and think about when and where you're most often tempted. Is it at certain times of the day? In certain places? After you do certain things? See certain people?

My internal battle often took place at night. It was the hardest when I was alone in my bedroom and lying in bed. My mind would come alive. I recognized that evening time was a struggle for me, so I began strategizing for that specific time of night. Instead of passively lying in bed and waiting for my mind to come alive, I would proactively begin praying. I would meditate on Scripture and write out verses. Sometimes I would jot down my thoughts and prayers in a journal. These were great ways for me to fight off temptation before it even hit (see 2 Tim. 2:22).

Identify when and where you struggle and then strategize for victory.

Of course, your strategy might look a little bit different. But the bottom line is this: identify when and where you struggle and then strategize for victory.

Pray

Prayer is one of the most powerful weapons you have (see 1 John 5:14–15). If you've accepted Christ as your personal Savior, the Holy Spirit is alive and active and living inside you. "Likewise the Spirit helps us in our weakness. For we do not know what to pray for as we ought, but the Spirit himself intercedes for us with groanings too deep for words" (Rom. 8:26).

The Holy Spirit is literally there to help you in your weaknesses. He is there to strengthen you and give you the victory.

Matthew 28:18–20 reminds us of an encouraging and hope-filled reality. "And Jesus came and said to them, 'All authority in heaven and on earth has been given to me. Go therefore and make disciples of all nations, baptizing them in the name of the Father and of the Son and of the Holy Spirit, teaching them to observe all that I have commanded you. And behold, I am with you always, to the end of age.'" You are not on your own in this battle. Thanks to God and His amazing mercy, you have access to His perfect strength through Jesus's death and resurrection as well as by the Spirit living within you (see Eph. 3:12). Take advantage of this amazing gift.

Here are two specific things you can pray for:

1. *Pray for yourself.* Cry out to God and ask Him to help you in your weakness. Ask Him to strengthen you and give you the power to honor Him inwardly. Ask Him to make you more like Jesus. Also, make prayer a regular part of your life and not just when you're struggling.

2. *Pray for other people.* One of the best ways to get your mind off the fantasy, the sexual thought, or the struggle is to pray for others. Your mind can only do so much at one time. If you're praying for other people, you won't have room to focus on your fantasy. This is a great way to fight the battle and serve others at the same time.

Inner Purity Is Possible

The battle for inner purity won't be quick and it won't be easy, but it is possible. The two of us have seen our own hearts radically changed. We've seen God transform us from gold-star Christian girls to women who passionately love Jesus. He can do the same for you. As you conform your mind to truth, your affections will follow and by God's grace you will find it easier to embrace a genuine heart of purity. When your goal is to love God with all that is within you, your outward actions will become an authentic reflection of what's taking place in your heart.

11. REAL TALK: PORN, EROTICA, AND MASTURBATION

With tears streaming down my (Kristen's) face, I sat on my bed feeling utterly hopeless. As a fifteen-year-old girl, my desire for sexual intimacy was strong and I felt as though I could hardly bear it anymore. In that moment, I wasn't sure how I would survive until marriage with such strong sexual desires. *How is this a gift?* I questioned God through my tears.

In my heart, I knew how much God valued purity and holiness, but it seemed impossible to consistently resist my urges for any length of time. I tried to control my lustful thoughts, but they seemed to overpower me more regularly than not. Sexualized images and fantasies bombarded my mind at the most unexpected moments.

During this time, masturbation became an unwelcome yet consistent companion. The shame and guilt I felt after giving into my lust lingered like a heavy, dark cloud. I found myself on a roller coaster of winning the battle one week and losing it the next. I wanted victory so bad. *Why is this so hard?* I would cry out to God. I prayed for my desires

so has my hope from the LORD. . ."
But this I call to mind,
  and therefore I have hope:

The steadfast love of the LORD never ceases;
  his mercies never come to an end;
they are new every morning;
  great is your faithfulness.
"The LORD is my portion," says my soul,
  "therefore I will hope in him."

The LORD is good to those who wait for him,
  to the soul who seeks him. (Lam. 3:17–18, 21–25)

We pray you will cling to the truth of God's Word and believe that your abuser does not have the final say in your story. We pray you would begin, or continue, the process of believing that God can turn even the worst of evils into good for His glory. We pray you will believe the truth that you are a worthy woman because of Christ's worth placed upon you and that nothing and nobody can ever take that worth away.

Five Steps to True Freedom and Lasting Healing

This list of steps to true freedom and lasting healing is far from exhaustive, but it's a start.

1. Tell a Trusted Source, Get Help, and Get Safe

Your protection and safety needs to be at the forefront of your mind and at the top of your priority list. If you are currently in an unsafe or harmful situation, you need to get help. Do not keep your situation a secret, thinking it will just resolve itself. Depending on your specific situation, you may need someone to help you figure out if you should contact the authorities, find a counselor, or help you relocate to a different home. Please speak up and let a trusted source know what's going on. Find someone who can help you and guide you to next steps.

For those of you who are years past the abusive situation, the two of us still encourage you to get help. If you've never taken steps to heal from the situation, we encourage you to get both spiritual and professional help. Talking to a wise, trusted woman in your church would be a great place to start.

2. Remember That No One Can Take Away Your Worth

No one and no thing can ever take away your worth. The Creator (God) is the giver of worth. He designed you and therefore He defines what makes you valuable. Absolutely nowhere in Scripture will you ever see God assigning someone's worth based on who they are or what's been done to them. That mind-set just doesn't exist in Scripture. The truth about your worth is not found in your opinion of yourself or anyone else's opinion of you. The truth about your worth is found in the perfect and timeless Word of God.

The following verses describe who you are and where your value comes from. If you are a born-again Christian, you are a beloved child of God. You are His. He has adopted you into His family and given you a new name—a child of God. That is your truest identity. You are fearfully and wonderfully made by your loving Father. Nothing done to your body can change the fact that God says you are His wonderfully created work. Don't let anyone tell you differently.

> For you formed my inward parts;
> you knitted me together in my mother's womb.

I praise you, for I am fearfully and wonderfully made.
Wonderful are your works;
    my soul knows it very well.
My frame was not hidden from you,
when I was being made in secret,
        intricately woven in the depths of the earth.
Your eyes saw my unformed substance;
in your book were written, every one of them,
    the days that were formed for me,
    when as yet there was none of them.
            (Ps. 139:13–16)

But to all who did receive him, who believed in his name, he gave the right to become children of God. (John 1:12)

Blessed be the God and Father of our Lord Jesus Christ, who has blessed us in Christ with every spiritual blessing in the heavenly places, even as he chose us in him before the foundation of the world, that we should be holy and blameless before him. In love he predestined us for adoption to himself as sons through Jesus Christ, according to the purpose of his will, to the praise of his glorious grace, with which he has blessed us in the Beloved. In him we have redemption through his blood, the forgiveness of our trespasses, according to the riches of his grace, which he lavished upon us, in all wisdom and insight. (Eph. 1:3–8)

3. Believe You Still Have a Future

The enemy would love for you to think that your life is over. He wants you to believe the lie that you are done. That you can't do any good or be used by God in any way. Those are lies straight from the pit of hell. God is in the redemption business and He delights in using those of us who feel weak to do mighty things for His kingdom. If God has you alive and breathing, it's because He has a purpose for your future. There are dozens of stories throughout the Bible of people who had been wronged, or done wrong, who God redeemed and used to accomplish amazing things! Think of Joseph (who we talked about previously), Esther, Moses, Bathsheba, Rahab, and Ruth. Each one of these individuals experienced difficult and traumatic life circumstances. Yet God still used each of them in incredible ways.

Think about the words Joseph said to His brothers and make them your own. "As for you, you meant evil against me, but God meant it for good, to bring it about that many people should be kept alive, as they are today" (Gen. 50:20). God used Joseph's broken past to bring forth life and hope for many, many people in the future. God wants to transform your past into a source of life-giving hope for others as well. He wants to use your journey as a testimony of His transforming grace and power.

Remember that God truly can take what was meant for evil against you and turn it into good. That is a miraculous hope you can hold on to.

> And we know that for those who love God all things work together for good, for those who are called according to his purpose. For those whom he foreknew he also predestined to be conformed to the image of his Son, in order that he might be the firstborn among many brothers. (Rom. 8: 28–29)

4. Trust That God Is Bigger Than This

God isn't limited in His power to redeem us. He can restore us from the darkest circumstances and lowest places. Trust that God sees your circumstances and that He cares. God knows about the abuse you suffered, but He doesn't condone it. He hates sexual abuse. He hates all evil. He will bring about justice on those who do evil (see Rom. 12:19).

God sent Jesus to die so that one day we will be permanently restored with Him in glory. Trust that God is bigger than the abuse in your life. Trust that He can do a mighty work in your heart and give you peace that surpasses all understanding.

The Bible tells us there's fullness of joy in God's presence and He has given us everything we need for life and godliness (see Ps. 16). In His presence, you can find peace and rest. Learning to trust Him fully is the very best thing you can do for your heart and soul.

> You make known to me the path of life;
>   in your presence there is fullness of joy;
>   at your right hand are pleasures forevermore.
>   (Ps. 16:11)

> Trust in the LORD with all your heart,
>   and do not lean on your own understanding.
> In all your ways acknowledge him,
>   and he will make straight your paths. (Prov. 3:5–6)

His divine power has granted to us all things that pertain to life and godliness, through the knowledge of him who called us to his own glory and excellence. (2 Pet. 1:3)

5. Surround Yourself with Genuine, Loving Christians

Letting people into the vulnerable places of your life can be difficult. It can be hard to know who to trust and who to open up to. But don't let these things stop you from having authentic community. You need genuine, loving Christians to support you during this time. Start by finding one older, genuine Christian woman who can be a friend and mentor.

Allow her into the deepest places of your life and begin building a friendship with her. Be honest and open. Give her the opportunity to encourage you. When you're struggling or giving into despair, ask her to pray for you. Don't try to heal on your own.

> And let us consider how to stir up one another to love and good works, not neglecting to meet together, as is the habit of some, but encouraging one another, and all the more as you see the Day drawing near. (Heb. 10:24–25)

> Put on then, as God's chosen ones, holy and beloved, compassionate hearts, kindness, humility, meekness, and patience, bearing with one another and, if one has a complaint against another, forgiving each other; as the Lord has forgiven you, so you also must forgive. And above all these put on love, which binds everything together in perfect harmony. (Col. 3:12–14)

Abuse Does Not Have the Final Say

Remember that abuse does not have the final say in your story. Hopelessness is not your destiny. God can restore, redeem, and turn your ashes into beauty. The two of us pray God will grant you His true peace that surpasses all understanding. We pray God will do a mighty healing work in your heart and help you reclaim your true identity as His beloved daughter.

As we mentioned previously, there is so much information to cover on this topic, and we've only scratched the surface. We encourage you to look into the following resources and set aside some time to explore them. Filling your heart and mind with biblical truth is crucial in guiding you toward true healing and lasting change.

Recommended Books

Pamela Gannon and Beverly Moore, *In the Aftermath: Past the Pain of Childhood Sexual Abuse* (Bemidji, MN: Focus, 2017).

Justin Halcomb and Lindsey Halcomb, *Rid of My Disgrace: Hope and Healing for Victims of Sexual Assault* (Wheaton: Crossway, 2001).

Robert W. Kellermen, *Sexual Abuse: Beauty for Ashes (Gospel for Real Life)* (Philipsburg, NJ: P&R, 2013).

David Powlison, *Making All Things New: Restoring Joy to the Sexually Broken* (Wheaton: Crossway, 2017).

Recommended Websites

www.biblicalcounseling.org
www.desiringgod.org

DISCUSSION QUESTIONS

Chapter 1: WE'RE ALL SEXUALLY BROKEN

"Regardless of your background, upbringing, race, or age, sexual brokenness is something every person faces."

1. In what ways have you been "discipled" by the world's view of sexuality?
2. What has been most influential—negative or positive—in shaping your current perspective of sexuality?
3. In what ways have you felt alone in your struggles with sexual sin?
4. Read Isaiah 61:3. What does God want to do with your heart and mind?
5. What are you most hoping to gain by reading this book?

Chapter 2: LUST: A GIRL'S PROBLEM TOO

"Despite the fact that many of us, as women, have felt like we're the only ones who struggle with lust, we're anything but alone."

1. Does your sexual design feel more like a curse or a blessing? Why?
2. In what ways have you seen lust most often presented as a guy issue?
3. Which one of the differences between men and women was most insightful to you?
4. Read Genesis 1:27. What does this verse teach you about sexuality?
5. John Piper describes lust as being void of holiness toward God and honor toward another person. How does that description of lust apply to both men and women?
6. To change the narrative about lust, we need to get honest with ourselves and with others. We need to begin talking about our struggles and share openly with other women. Take a moment right now to get honest. What lustful struggles have you wrestled with that need to be brought into the light?

Chapter 3: WHEN EVERYTHING RIGHT WENT WRONG

"Sexuality has been so chopped up, reshaped, and altered that it looks very different from what God originally designed it to be."

1. The way we navigate our sexuality today is similar to someone trying to put together an extremely complex puzzle without the photo on the box to guide them. What source do you most often turn to for help in navigating questions about sexuality?
2. What's the difference between sexual instinct and sexual intimacy?

3. How should God's intentional design for the male and the female in Genesis inform our view of sexuality?
4. Read Genesis 2:25. Why were Adam and Eve both naked and unashamed?
5. Our eyes wander and our hearts question—just as Eve's did. In what ways do you struggle to trust God's truth for sexuality?
6. How have you seen sin impact sexuality in modern society?

Chapter 4: FOUR CULTURAL LIES ABOUT OUR SEXUAL DESIGN

"When we choose to embrace anything but God's good and original design for our sexuality, we buy into an inaccurate reflection of who God created us to be."

1. In what ways have you seen society cheapen and devalue sexual intimacy?
2. Answering from a biblical perspective, why wouldn't our society's moral relativism be a sign of advancement rather than a sign of foolishness and pride?
3. Thinking back on the four lies of our sexual design, in what ways have you been influenced to buy into Lie #1 (Sexual Identity Is Determined by Personal Desires)?
4. The contrast between *Merriam-Webster's* 1828 definition of *marriage* and the modern definition is shocking. What stood out to you when you compared these definitions side by side?
5. The advice *Teen Vogue* is giving to young women regarding sex is simply "If it feels right, do it." Although this

advice sounds good, in what ways does it undermine God's design for sex?

6. How have you seen modern femininity portrayed as powerful and seductive?

Chapter 5: THE HERO EVERY WOMAN NEEDS

"Jesus is the true hero who every one of us desperately needs."

1. In what ways have you related to stories about a hero rescuing a struggler?
2. Read Genesis 3:21. Why weren't Adam's and Eve's fig leaves a sufficient covering for them?
3. Read John 3:16. According to this verse, how does Jesus act as your hero?
4. In what ways have you pretended to be enough before God?
5. Galatians 2:20 says, "I have been crucified with Christ. It is no longer I who live, but Christ who lives in me. And the life I now live in the flesh I live by faith in the Son of God, who loved me and gave himself for me." How does this verse apply to your life?
6. How does Kate's story of struggle and victory encourage you?
7. What inner struggles are you wrestling with that you need to pour out to God in prayer?

Chapter 6: FOUR BIBLICAL TRUTHS ABOUT OUR SEXUAL DESIGN

"In a world of confusing messages and ever-evolving definitions, God's Word is constant. His design for our sexuality, which He established at the beginning of creation, hasn't changed from the beginning of Creation."

1. What you believe about God's Word will directly affect your view of sexuality. At this point in time, which type of woman are you most like: Denier Girl, Cherry-Picker Girl, or Accepter Girl?

2. Read John 8:32 out loud. What do you think it means to be set free by God's truth?

3. Thinking back on the four truths of our sexual design, what stood out to you the most about Jackie Hill Perry's testimony in Truth #1 (Sexual Identity Is a God-Assigned Reality)?

4. Read Ephesians 5:22–24. In Truth #2 (Marriage Is a Covenant between a Man and a Woman), we talked about the fact that God's greatest purpose for creating marriage is to show the world an earthly representation of what Christ's covenant relationship looks like with His Church. How should this biblical reality shape your view of marriage?

5. In Truth #3 (Sex Was Created for Intimacy within Marriage), we talked about how God created our sexual desires to push us toward an intimate relationship with Him. What did you find most eye-opening about this biblical truth?

6. Read Proverbs 9:1–18. In Truth #4 (Femininity Is a Display of God's Design for Womanhood), we examined

the picture of "wisdom" and "folly" displayed through the narrative of two women. What changes do you need to make in your life to reflect lady wisdom?

7. Of the four truths discussed in this chapter, which one do you most need God's help with in wholeheartedly embracing?

Chapter 7: GIRL, YOU WERE MADE FOR INTIMACY

"We were made for yada. We were made for deep intimacy with Jesus. When our hearts are filled with a soul-satisfying relationship with Jesus, we have everything we need to thrive."

1. In what ways have you experienced a lack of yada in your relationships (both romantic and non-romantic)?

2. As we saw in this chapter, the word *yada* is used 940 times in the Old Testament and in Hebrew literally means "to know deeply or intimately." What do you think it means to know (yada) God in this way?

3. Read Psalm 139:1, 13, 14. Each time the word *know* is used, say the word *yada* out loud. How does this change your understanding of these verses?

4. How does yada expand your view of sexual intimacy?

5. Single women: Why is an authentic relationship with Jesus the most important thing you can pursue?

6. Married women: In what ways have you seen the relational and emotional aspects of yada impact the state of your sexual relationship within marriage?

Chapter 8: IMPERFECT PURITY

"[Sexual purity is] ultimately about embracing your identity as a daughter of God and striving every day to become more like Him."

1. When you hear the word *purity*, what is the first thing that comes to mind?
2. Why is it important to have a biblical understanding of God's design for purity?
3. According to Wrong Narrative #1 (Sex Is a Bad and Scary Thing), why is sex portrayed as a bad and scary thing?
4. Why is Wrong Narrative #2 (Your Worth Is Based on Your Level of Pureness) an anti-gospel message?
5. Read Romans 5:8. How does this verse impact your view of purity?
6. Wrong Narrative #3 says that purity is only for single people. Describe why this is simply not true.
7. A biblical narrative of purity says a heart that desires to honor God must be the foundation for purity. In what ways do you need to change your perspective of purity to align with a biblical perspective?

Chapter 9: BATTLING TEMPTATION

"Temptation draws our hearts and minds away from glorifying God and toward satisfying our own sinful desires. It encourages us to question God's authority and consider the possibility of a better way."

1. Thinking about your own life, when was the last time you were faced with sexual temptation?

2. In your own words, describe what you think this statement means: "To be forewarned of Satan's strategy is to be forearmed."

3. Thinking back on the six biblical facts about temptation (see pages 115–16), which one did you find most eye-opening or helpful?

4. Read James 1:13–16. Describe a time in your life when you followed the pattern of temptation by listening, pondering, and then accepting the alluring offer of sin.

5. Thinking back on Joseph's incredible example of running from temptation (see Gen. 39:1–23), how does his story of victory encourage you in your fight against temptation?

6. Now that you understand the three-step process of temptation, how can you practically apply it in your everyday life?

Chapter 10: THE SECRET STRUGGLE WITHIN YOUR MIND

"Our goal isn't just to achieve a status of purity, but to align our entire lives, inner and outer, with the great and first commandment in the Bible . . . to love the Lord our God with all our hearts, souls, and minds."

1. Describe a time in your life when you looked "pure" on the outside but were secretly struggling with lustful sin on the inside.

2. The secret battle within the mind is something everyone faces. Thinking back to the secret struggle heart check (see page 129), which of the areas are you wrestling with most right now?

3. Read Psalm 139:2–4. What do these verses teach you about God and His understanding of your secret inner struggles?

4. How does your understanding of the mind, affections, and will (see pages 130–32) help you better battle internal lust?

5. Think back through the five strategies to help you fight inner struggle (purge, study, memorize, strategize, and pray). Which of these five strategies stood out to you the most and how can you begin putting it into action today?

Chapter 11: REAL TALK: PORN, EROTICA, AND MASTURBATION

"Whether you're struggling with masturbation, porn, erotica, or something else, you can find lasting freedom in Christ."

1. What sexual struggles have you wrestled with (now or in the past) that felt too big to overcome?

2. We serve a powerful God, and no sin is too great for the cross of our Savior to conquer. How did Kristen's story of struggle and victory encourage you in your own fight?

3. When looking at the four reasons for why porn is a counterfeit version of true intimacy, which one stood out to you the most and why?

   • Porn is a mockery of covenant love.
   • Porn degrades God's image bearers.
   • Porn warps our longings and desires.
   • Porn is a form of false worship.

4. Take a moment to read each of the following verses: Psalm 51:10; 1 Corinthians 6:18; and 1 Thessalonians 4:3–5. In light of God's truth, why is erotica an unhelpful and unwise choice for Christian women?

5. When looking at the three reasons why masturbation is a counterfeit version of true intimacy, which one stood out to you the most and why?

- Masturbation promotes isolation and selfishness.
- Masturbation is often fueled by lust.
- Masturbation fails to bring God glory.

6. Regardless of how strong and overwhelming your sexual urges and desires may be at times, you must believe that God's grace is sufficient to help you. How can you apply Galatians 5:16 ("But I say, walk by the Spirit, and you will not gratify the desires of the flesh") to your life right now?

7. Your journey toward sexual freedom can begin today. Which of the following four steps toward freedom do you need to humbly engage in today?

- Pursue genuine repentance.
- Bring secret sins into the light.
- Seek ongoing discipleship from a godly woman.
- Make radical changes.

Chapter 12: ANSWERING THE HUSH-HUSH QUESTIONS

"Be bold in chasing down truth. Continue thinking deeply and searching for biblical answers to every hush-hush question."

1. If you could add any hush-hush question to this chapter, what question would you add?

2. When it comes to your secret hush-hush questions, where do you typically turn for answers?

3. Why do you think it's important to find biblically grounded answers to our secret questions?

4. Read 2 Timothy 3:16–17. What do these verses teach us about pursuing truth?

5. Take some time to think of a godly Titus 2 woman in your life. What action steps can you take to connect with her and ask her your questions?

Chapter 13: SEXUAL FREEDOM THAT LASTS

"God calls us to live a new life in Christ. A life free from the grip of sexual sin."

1. In what ways have you found yourself in a cycle of temptation and failure?

2. Why isn't "trying harder" the solution for long-term and lasting change?

3. Read 1 John 1:9. According to that verse, what does God promise to do for you?

4. How does the illustration about clothing (see pages 178–80) relate to spiritually growing and changing?

5. Read Ephesians 4:20–24. Unpack the three steps discussed in this passage. How should those steps impact the way you approach spiritual growth?

6. In what ways is the Christian life like running a marathon?

Chapter 14: FINALLY SATISFIED

"Finding satisfaction in Christ must be our ultimate pursuit. If we, as women, want to experience the true pleasures Christ can offer, we have to look to Him."

1. Think of one person who you really, really love (e.g., spouse, sibling, friend, parent, etc.). What do you do to pursue and cherish that relationship?
2. With that person in mind, what would it look like if you treasured and cherished your relationship with Christ in the same way?
3. In what ways have you pursued "earthly treasure" only to be left dissatisfied and empty in the end?
4. Read Psalm 16:11. How should this verse impact the way you pursue personal pleasure and satisfaction?
5. Of the three ideas offered for cherishing Christ (worship Him, pray through Scripture, journal your prayers), which one resonated with you the most?
6. If you could add an additional idea for treasuring Christ, what would it be?

Chapter 15: REDEEMED SEXUALITY

"Regardless of where you've been, what you've done, or what's been done to you, you are a redeemed woman in Christ, set apart for God's glory."

1. Explain why your sexual experiences (whether good or bad) do not define you.
2. Read Matthew 11:28. What does God say He will give to those who come to Him?
3. What does the powerful story of the prostitute (see pages 197–99) teach you about Jesus?
4. How have you seen God transform your ashes into beauty for His glory?
5. As you begin a new chapter in your journey, what specific prayers are you bringing before God?

ACKNOWLEDGMENTS

Writing a book on God's design for sexuality wasn't exactly a lifelong dream of ours . . . but when we saw the hundreds of emails flooding our inbox from the GirlDefined Sisterhood asking tough questions about sexuality, a fire was ignited within our hearts. When Baker Books offered us a third contract, we knew exactly what the book needed to be about—sex, purity, and the longings of a girl's heart. Although this book has been the most challenging and laborious one by far, it was well worth it. God's design for sexuality is powerful, beautiful, and incredibly freeing. As we've seen God's truth transform our own brokenness into beauty for His glory, we pray this book brings about the same transformation for each and every woman who reads it.

As always, this book wouldn't be what it is without the help, love, and support from our incredible family, friends, and team.

God . . . thank You first and foremost for giving us the opportunity to write this book and proclaim your goodness. Thank you for intentionally creating us as sexual beings in order to draw us into an intimate and soul-satisfying relationship with You.

Dad and Mom . . . our lifelong supporters and biggest fans. Thank you for being there for us, yet again! You never seem to grow weary of cheering us on, and we're grateful for that. We love you!

Zack . . . our all-around go-to guy, technology guru, and constant high-fiver. Thank you for encouraging us on those many late nights when we'd sit at the kitchen table, slumped over, trying to finish "one more chapter." You're the best.

Dāv . . . no one can beat your energy and enthusiasm. Your spontaneous songs, impromptu cheers of encouragement, and epic dance moves kept us smiling and energized throughout this entire writing process. Welcome to the family!

Our awesome siblings . . . you kept us going with the surprise coffee drop-offs, fresh cookies, and constant reminders that we could do it.

Mershon family . . . your constant prayers and encouragement were priceless. We absolutely loved the surprise visits to snuggle with Hadley, Willa, and Ellis. We're some very blessed aunts!

The entire Clark family . . . thanks for always being there for us during each book-writing project. Your prayers, words of encouragement, and overall interest in our books always give us the boost we need.

The Beal family . . . thank you for being so supportive and encouraging during Bethany's visits to Idaho while in the midst of an intense writing deadline. Y'all are the sweetest.

GirlDefined Prayer Team . . . your prayers were answered, and this book is the proof. We treasure each one of you.

The elders at Crossway Bible Church . . . thank you for taking the time to review an advance copy of this manuscript. Your godly wisdom and biblical insight was invaluable.

Nicci Jordan Hubert . . . you are an incredible editor. Thank you for sticking with us and pouring your time and energy into this book. Your insights were game changers. This book is sharper, stronger, and more grace-filled because of you.

Rebekah Guzman . . . again, thank you for believing in us and giving us the opportunity to write another book. We can't thank you enough!

Baker Books . . . your team is incredible. We have truly loved working with every single person at Baker. Thank you for working with us to publish a third book.

Friends who supported us along the way . . . thanks for sticking with us through yet another book. Now that it's finished, let's finally grab breakfast and a cup of delicious coffee.

NOTES

Chapter 1 We're All Sexually Broken

1. Dr. Juli Slattery, *Rethinking Sexuality: God's Design and Why It Matters* (Colorado Springs: Multnomah, 2018), 77.
2. Slattery, *Rethinking Sexuality*, 20.

Chapter 2 Lust: A Girl's Problem Too

1. John Piper, "Battling the Unbelief of Lust," Desiring God, November 13, 1988, https://www.desiringgod.org/messages/battling-the-unbelief-of-lust.

Chapter 4 Four Cultural Lies about Our Sexual Design

1. Dannah Gresh and Dr. Juli Slattery, *Pulling Back the Shades* (Chicago: Moody, 2014), 71.
2. "Tube Sites Are Free, So How Does the Porn Industry Actually Make Money?," Fight the New Drug, June 20, 2018, https://fightthenewdrug.org/how-does-the-porn-industry-actually-make-money-today/.
3. "How Many People Are on Porn Sites Right Now? (Hint: It's a Lot.)," Fight the New Drug, April 2, 2018, https://fightthenewdrug.org/by-the-numbers-see-how-many-people-are-watching-porn-today/.
4. Vera Papisova, "Find Out When Most Teens Are Losing Their Virginity," *Teen Vogue*, September 30, 2015, https://www.teenvogue.com/story/teens-losing-virginity-age.
5. "Sexual Orientation," Planned Parenthood, accessed September 21, 2018, https://www.plannedparenthood.org/learn/sexual-orientation-gender/sexual-orientation.

6. Owen Strachan, "The Clarity of Complementarity: Gender Dysphoria in Biblical Perspective," Council on Biblical Manhood and Womanhood, April 25, 2017, https://cbmw.org/topics/complementarianism/the-clarity-of-complementarity-gender-dysphoria-in-biblical-perspective/.

7. *Merriam-Webster*, s.v. "Marriage," accessed September 21, 2018, https://www.merriam-webster.com/dictionary/marriage.

8. *Merriam-Webster*, s.v. "Marriage."

9. "Marriage," *Psychology Today*, accessed September 21, 2018, https://www.psychologytoday.com/us/basics/marriage.

10. Webster's Dictionary 1828 Online, s.v. "Marriage," accessed September 21, 2018, http://webstersdictionary1828.com/Dictionary/marriage.

11. Kaleigh Fasanella, "How to Decide If You're Ready for Sex," *Teen Vogue*, October 21, 2016, https://www.teenvogue.com/story/how-to-know-if-you-are-ready-to-have-sex.

Chapter 5 The Hero Every Woman Needs

1. John Piper, "What Is the Christian Gospel?," Desiring God, June 5, 2002, https://www.desiringgod.org/articles/what-is-the-christian-gospel.

Chapter 6 Four Biblical Truths about Our Sexual Design

1. Leigh Montville, "Trials of David," *Sports Illustrated*, April 29, 1996, 95.

2. C. S. Lewis, *The Weight of Glory* (San Francisco: HarperOne, 2015), 27.

3. John Piper, "Genitalia Are Not Destiny—But Are They Design?," Desiring God, June 2, 2014, https://www.desiringgod.org/articles/genitalia-are-not-destiny-but-are-they-design.

4. Christopher Asmus, "Longing for Intimacy," Desiring God, January 18, 2018, https://www.desiringgod.org/articles/longing-for-intimacy.

5. Asmus, "Longing for Intimacy."

6. Rosaria Champagne Butterfield, "Is Sexual Orientation a Concept That Christians Ought to Use?," www.rosariabutterfield.com, accessed October 30, 2018, https://rosariabutterfield.com/new-blog/2018/2/14/is-sexual-orientation-a-concept-that-christians-ought-to-use.

7. Jackie Hill Perry, "Love Letter to a Lesbian," Desiring God, July 20, 2013, https://www.desiringgod.org/articles/love-letter-to-a-lesbian.

8. Jasmine Holmes, "Q&A: Jackie Hill Perry on 'Bending Myself to Jesus,'" *Christianity Today*, May 24, 2018, https://www.christianitytoday.com/women/2018/may/q-and-jackie-hill-perry-bending-myself-to-jesus-rap.html.

9. Piper, "Genitalia Are Not Destiny."

10. Tim Challies, "What's the Purpose of . . . Marriage?," www.challies .com, September 8, 2017, https://www.challies.com/articles/whats-the -purpose-of-marriage/.

11. Kristen Clark and Bethany Baird, *Love Defined: Embracing God's Vision for Lasting Love and Satisfying Relationships* (Grand Rapids: Baker Books, 2018), 72.

12. Challies, "What's the Purpose of . . . Marriage?"

13. Wandering MGTOW, "Is Sex Completely Boring to Anyone Else?," Men Going Their Own Way, July 8, 2015, https://www.mgtow.com/forums /topic/is-sex-completely-boring-to-anyone-else/.

14. Garrett Kell, "Good Lovemaking Is about God," Desiring God, July 11, 2017, https://www.desiringgod.org/articles/good-lovemaking-is -about-god.

15. Dr. Juli Slattery, *Rethinking Sexuality: God's Design and Why It Matters* (Colorado Springs: Multnomah, 2018), 53, 58.

16. Dr. Juli Slattery, "Sex and the Single Girl with Dr. Juli Slattery," YouTube.com, accessed September 24, 2018, https://www.youtube.com /watch?v=TP8eUerN4Cw&t=3s.

17. Slattery, "Sex and the Single Girl."

18. Timothy J. Keller, "Love and Lust" (sermon, Redeemer Presbyterian Church, New York, May 6, 2012), www.gospelinlife.com/downloads /love-and-lust-6151.

19. Slattery, *Rethinking Sexuality*, 55–56.

20. Dannah Gresh, "A Modest Proposal for My Critics," Pure Freedom, March 12, 2013, http://purefreedom.org/a-modest-proposal-to-my -critics/.

21. Gresh, "Modest Proposal."

Chapter 7 Girl, You Were Made for Intimacy

1. Dr. Juli Slattery, "Why Does Sex Matter?," Authentic Intimacy, March 9, 2015, https://www.authenticintimacy.com/resources/3028/why -does-sex-matter.

2. Jon Bloom, "How to Have Intimacy with God," Desiring God, January 29, 2016, https://www.desiringgod.org/articles/how-to-have -intimacy-with-god.

3. Greg Smalley, "Does 'Yada, Yada, Yada' in Your Marriage Mean It's 'Blah, Blah, Blah'?," Focus on the Family, accessed September 24, 2018, https://www.focusonthefamily.com/marriage/sex-and-intimacy/does -yada-yada-yada-in-your-marriage-mean-its-blah-blah-blah.

4. Smalley, "Does 'Yada, Yada, Yada' in Your Marriage?"

Chapter 8 Imperfect Purity

1. Dr. Juli Slattery, "Why the Word *Purity* Is Cringy," Authentic Intimacy, November 8, 2017, https://www.authenticintimacy.com/resources/6815/purity.

Chapter 9 Battling Temptation

1. Steven J. Cole, "Lesson 8: How Temptation Works (Genesis 3:1–7)," Bible.org, accessed September 21, 2018, https://bible.org/seriespage/lesson-8-how-temptation-works-genesis-31-7.
2. John Owen, *Temptation: Resisted and Repulsed* (Carlisle, PA: The Banner of Truth Trust, 2007), 10–11.
3. Nancy DeMoss Wolgemuth, *Lies Women Believe: And the Truth That Sets Them Free* (Chicago: Moody, 2001), 38.
4. Dan Armstrong, "The 4 Stages of Temptation," covenanteyes.com, February 26, 2016, http://www.covenanteyes.com/2016/02/26/the-four-stages-of-temptation/.
5. Armstrong, "The 4 Stages."

Chapter 10 The Secret Struggle within Your Mind

1. Elyse Fitzpatrick, *Idols of the Heart: Learning to Long for God Alone* (Phillipsburg, NJ: P&R, 2016); 104–7
2. Fitzpatrick, *Idols*, 104–7.

Chapter 11 Real Talk: Porn, Erotica, and Masturbation

1. "18 Mind-Blowing Stats about the Porn Industry and Its Underage Consumers," fightthenewdrug.org, accessed September 24, 2018, https://fightthenewdrug.org/10-porn-stats-that-will-blow-your-mind/.
2. "18 Mind-Blowing Stats."
3. Jill Hamilton, "The 12 Best Porn Movies Money Can Buy," *Cosmopolitan*, March 16, 2018, https://www.cosmopolitan.com/sex-love/g19460176/best-porn-movies/.
4. Luke Gilkerson, "Brain Chemicals and Porn Addiction: Science Shows How Porn Harms Us," covenanteyes.com, February 3, 2014, http://www.covenanteyes.com/2014/02/03/brain-chemicals-and-porn-addiction/.
5. Christopher Asmus, "Why Do We Give In to Porn?," Desiring God, July 31, 2017, https://www.desiringgod.org/articles/why-do-we-give-in-to-porn.
6. Trip Lee, "Hope and Help for the Porn Addict," Desiring God, June 30, 2015, https://www.desiringgod.org/articles/hope-and-help-for-the-porn-addict.
7. Asmus, "Why Do We Give In?"

8. Dannah Gresh and Dr. Juli Slattery, *Pulling Back the Shades* (Chicago: Moody, 2014), 9.

9. Gresh and Slattery, *Pulling Back*, 18.

10. Dannah Gresh, "I Know Why You Read Fifty Shades of Grey," Pure Freedom, February 27, 2014, http://purefreedom.org/i-know-why-you-read-fifty-shades-of-grey/.

11. Gresh and Slattery, *Pulling Back*, 18.

12. Dannah Gresh, "I'm Not Reading Fifty Shades of Grey," Pure Freedom, January 7, 2013, http://purefreedom.org/im-not-reading-fifty-shades-of-grey/.

13. Dictionary.com, s.v. "Masturbation," accessed September 24, 2018, https://www.dictionary.com/browse/masturbation.

14. Tim Challies, "God's Truth on Your Secret Sexual Sin," Revive Our Hearts, accessed September 24, 2018, https://www.reviveourhearts.com/articles/gods-truth-your-secret-sexual-sin/.

15. Challies, "God's Truth."

16. Jason DeRouchie, "If Your Right Hand Causes You to Sin," Desiring God, December 3, 2016, https://www.desiringgod.org/articles/if-your-right-hand-causes-you-to-sin.

17. Lauren Jacobs, "Ashamed, Alone, and Addicted to Porn: Do Other Women Struggle with This?," covenanteyes.com, November 9, 2012, http://www.covenanteyes.com/2012/11/09/women-addicted-to-porn-lauren-jacobs/.

18. Joshua Harris, *Sex Is Not the Problem (Lust Is)* (Colorado Springs: Multnomah, 2003), 43.

Chapter 12 Answering the Hush-Hush Questions

1. Kristen Clark and Bethany Baird, *Love Defined: Embracing God's Vision for Lasting Love and Satisfying Relationships* (Grand Rapids: Baker Books, 2018), 189.

2. Heath Lambert, "A Personal Statement on Abuse," Association of Certified Biblical Counselors, May 8, 2018, https://biblicalcounseling.com/2018/05/abuse/.

3. Clark and Baird, *Love Defined*, 213.

Chapter 13 Sexual Freedom That Lasts

1. Heath Lambert, *Finally Free: Fighting for Purity with the Power of Grace* (Grand Rapids: Zondervan, 2013), 28.

2. Lambert, *Finally Free*, 21.

3. Lambert, *Finally Free*, 21.

4. Joshua Harris, *Sex Is Not the Problem (Lust Is)* (Colorado Springs: Multnomah, 2003), 27.

5. Steve Viars, "Learning How to Grow—Ephesians 4:22–24," Faith Church, August 28, 1990, https://www.faithlafayette.org/resources/lessons/learning_how_to_grow_ephesians_422_24.

Chapter 14 Finally Satisfied

1. Phillip Holmes, "Only Christ Can Truly Satisfy," Desiring God, October 8, 2015, https://www.desiringgod.org/articles/only-christ-can-truly-satisfy.
2. John Piper, "There Is No Greater Satisfaction," Desiring God, October 1, 1990, https://www.desiringgod.org/articles/there-is-no-greater-satisfaction.
3. Reginald Heber, "Holy, Holy, Holy," 1826.
4. Holmes, "Only Christ Can Truly Satisfy."

Chapter 15 Redeemed Sexuality

1. Jon Bloom, "Breaking the Power of Shame," Desiring God, July 15, 2016, https://www.desiringgod.org/articles/breaking-the-power-of-shame.

Appendix: Finding Hope and Healing from Sexual Abuse

1. "Statistics," Center for Family Justice, last accessed November 29, 2018, https://centerforfamilyjustice.org/community-education/statistics/.
2. Dawn Wilson, "Trusting God to Heal the Scars of Sexual Abuse," Revive our Hearts, February 16, 2017, https://www.reviveourhearts.com/true-woman/blog/sexual-abuse-trusting-god-with-my-past-hurts/.
3. Kathleen Shumate, "God Can Overcome Any Abuse," Desiring God, April 27, 2017, https://www.desiringgod.org/articles/god-can-overcome-any-abuse.
4. Paul Maxwell, "Trauma Is Not a Life Sentence," Desiring God, January 5, 2017, https://www.desiringgod.org/articles/trauma-is-not-a-life-sentence.

Kristen Clark is married to her best friend and forever crush, Zack. She is the cofounder of GirlDefined Ministries and coauthor of *Girl Defined* and *Love Defined*. She is passionate about promoting the message of biblical womanhood through blogging, speaking, mentoring young women, and hosting Bible studies in her living room. In the end, she's just a fun-lovin' Texas girl who adores all things outdoors and eats dark chocolate whenever possible.

Bethany Beal is married to her favorite person in the world, Dāv. She is the cofounder of GirlDefined Ministries and coauthor of *Girl Defined* and *Love Defined*. She is passionate about spreading the truth of biblical womanhood through blogging, speaking, and mentoring young women. To her family and close friends, she is simply a tall blonde girl who loves hosting game nights, is obsessed with smoothie bowls, and can't get enough of her little fluffy dog.